T0215546

Systematic Cloud Migration

A Hands-On Guide to Architecture, Design, and Technical Implementation

Taras Gleb

Apress®

Systematic Cloud Migration: A Hands-On Guide to Architecture, Design, and Technical Implementation

Taras Gleb
Thornhill, ON, Canada

ISBN-13 (pbk): 978-1-4842-7251-0   ISBN-13 (electronic): 978-1-4842-7252-7
https://doi.org/10.1007/978-1-4842-7252-7

Copyright © 2021 by Taras Gleb

This work is subject to copyright. All rights are reserved by the Publisher, whether the whole or part of the material is concerned, specifically the rights of translation, reprinting, reuse of illustrations, recitation, broadcasting, reproduction on microfilms or in any other physical way, and transmission or information storage and retrieval, electronic adaptation, computer software, or by similar or dissimilar methodology now known or hereafter developed.

Trademarked names, logos, and images may appear in this book. Rather than use a trademark symbol with every occurrence of a trademarked name, logo, or image we use the names, logos, and images only in an editorial fashion and to the benefit of the trademark owner, with no intention of infringement of the trademark.

The use in this publication of trade names, trademarks, service marks, and similar terms, even if they are not identified as such, is not to be taken as an expression of opinion as to whether or not they are subject to proprietary rights.

While the advice and information in this book are believed to be true and accurate at the date of publication, neither the authors nor the editors nor the publisher can accept any legal responsibility for any errors or omissions that may be made. The publisher makes no warranty, express or implied, with respect to the material contained herein.

Managing Director, Apress Media LLC: Welmoed Spahr
Acquisitions Editor: Susan McDermott
Development Editor: Laura Berendson
Coordinating Editor: Shrikant Vishwakarma

Cover designed by eStudioCalamar

Cover image designed by Pexels

Distributed to the book trade worldwide by Springer Science+Business Media LLC, 1 New York Plaza, Suite 4600, New York, NY 10004. Phone 1-800-SPRINGER, fax (201) 348-4505, e-mail orders-ny@springer-sbm.com, or visit www.springeronline.com. Apress Media, LLC is a California LLC and the sole member (owner) is Springer Science + Business Media Finance Inc (SSBM Finance Inc). SSBM Finance Inc is a **Delaware** corporation.

For information on translations, please e-mail booktranslations@springernature.com; for reprint, paperback, or audio rights, please e-mail bookpermissions@springernature.com, or visit http://www.apress.com/rights-permissions.

Apress titles may be purchased in bulk for academic, corporate, or promotional use. eBook versions and licenses are also available for most titles. For more information, reference our Print and eBook Bulk Sales web page at http://www.apress.com/bulk-sales.

Any source code or other supplementary material referenced by the author in this book is available to readers on GitHub via the book's product page, located at www.apress.com/978-1-4842-7251-0. For more detailed information, please visit http://www.apress.com/source-code.

Printed on acid-free paper

This book is dedicated to my wonderful children: to my son Nikita and my daughter Ivanka, with much love who showed me the path to pure, unclouded wisdom and boundless curiosity on all things around us.

Table of Contents

Conventions Used in This Book

The following typographical conventions are used in this book:

- *Italic* – Used for new terms, URLs, directories, email addresses, filenames, and file extensions.

- `Constant width` - Used for program listings, as well as within paragraphs to refer to program elements such as variable and function names, databases, data types, environment variables, statements, and keywords.

- **`Constant width bold`** – Used for commands or other text that should be typed literally by the user.

- *`Constant width italic`* - Shows text that should be replaced with user-supplied values or by values determined by context.

The following text blocks elements are used in this book:

- TIP - This element signifies a tip or suggestions.

- NOTE - This element signifies a general note.

- WARNING - This element indicates warning or caution.

- IMPORTANT - This element indicates important information.

About the Author

Taras Gleb is a pragmatic and hands-on cloud solutions architect focused on software delivery, strategy, and innovations. He has led software development and digital transformation projects in the areas of business applications, big data, reporting, machine learning, DevSecOps, and automation. He has 25+ years of experience in design and implementation of mission-critical, customer-oriented software solutions for institutional investors, governments, insurance companies, banks, capital markets, and power utilities. While delivering these solutions, he applies advanced software architecture and development methodologies. His focus is on building cloud-native, secure, innovative, and cost-efficient solutions that deliver business value in an agile manner. Taras is a life-long learner who holds a Degree in Engineering, Master of Business Administration from Aspen University (Colorado, USA) as well as various industry development, architecture and project management certifications, including PMP from Project Management Institute. He is continuously searching for novel, innovative and efficient ways to apply the latest technologies and methodologies to software architecture, development, delivery and operations. You can reach Taras via LinkedIn at *www.linkedin.com/in/tgleb* or via email at *gleb_taras@yahoo.com*.

About the Technical Reviewer

Dwight Gunning lives in Toronto, Canada and works as a data scientist building data analytics and machine learning applications in the cloud for a US financial regulator.

He has prior direct experience in developing cloud software while working for IBM SmartCloud.

When he isn't coding side projects in Python, he spends his free time exploring trails in the greater Toronto area.

Acknowledgments

My first acknowledgements have to go to my wonderful children, Nikita and Ivanka, and their dedicated mother, Polina, who are my endless source of energy and inspiration on this fascinating journey.

This book couldn't have happened without the support and guidance from Susan McDermott, Laura Berendson, and Shrikant Vishwakarma, who provided me with the resources necessary to see the book through.

Specifically, I would like to thank my colleague and friend Dwight Gunning, who reviewed the book and provided insightful feedback that focused the content in some cases and reduced ambiguities in others.

Introduction

The emergence of cloud computing within the last two decades has brought ground-breaking innovations and related transformations to the information technology industry. It has revolutionized the way organizations develop, deliver, and operate software applications, as well as brought profound changes to supporting infrastructure, security, and enterprise services.

Well-implemented cloud computing strategy could be a competitive advantage and has already become a differentiating factor in the marketplace for many companies. Amazon, Microsoft, and Google are prime examples of such success. Conversely, cloud computing has also introduced numerous challenges that could lead to higher costs, increased complexity, and missed market opportunities. Hence, it is vital to understand what cloud computing is, what opportunities and challenges it presents, and how to ride the cloud computing wave to benefit your organization without drowning in it.

That's where this book comes in. Its objective is to serve as a comprehensive, coherent, and systematic cloud migration guide. Experiences shared in this book are drawn from real-life migration projects and contain practical advice, as well as step-by-step architecture, design, and technical implementation instructions using sample application code from GitHub. Following this book will provide much needed support to your teams, and help you successfully complete the application cloud migration journey.

Target Audience

This text is primarily designed with software developers, team leads, technical development managers, DevSecOps engineers, production support technicians, and software architects in mind. Their day-to-day activities include architecting, designing, developing, delivering, and operating software in the cloud environment. In addition, this book will benefit infrastructure, network, security, and operations engineers, who in turn, can provide better support for the software development product teams.

The book provides structured and deep insights into cloud-related characteristics, paradigm shifts, cloud-native tools, methodologies, and technologies, plus sound engineering and cost-efficient design techniques. You will find valuable insights that will help you identify cloud-related training requirements and help you develop the skillset to successfully migrate. These newly acquired skills will future-proof your technology career for years to come.

At the end of the day, this book aims to be your table-top reference guide. It provides straight migration advice and guides you to a solution as well as points you to carefully selected supplementary materials for additional research.

How This Book Is Structured

Organization of the book closely replicates the cloud migration process and is depicted in Figure 1. It is a result-oriented book that answers the *why, what, how, who,* and *when* of cloud migration. The text provides the teams with step-by-step instructions and ensures successful migration to the public cloud provider's infrastructure. The major parts are as follows:

- Part I: Introduction to Cloud Computing

- Part II: Software Development Migration

- Part III: Software Delivery Migration

- Part IV: Software Operations Migration

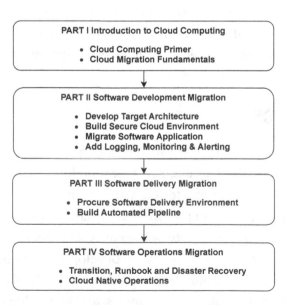

Figure 1. *Application Cloud Migration Structure*

Part I: Introduction to Cloud Computing

This part starts with an introduction to cloud computing and establishes a basic understanding of the different types of cloud computing characteristics. It lists business and technical motivational factors and benefits and explains cloud-native technologies and core paradigm changes within the application, infrastructure, delivery, operations, and security technology and service areas. In addition, it establishes and elaborates on major migration areas: software development (application code, data, infrastructure, security and configuration), software delivery (pipeline and automation), and software operations (observability, cost, and platform management). It concludes with an introduction to a high-level migration process, including major steps to be applied to each migration area. This blueprint becomes our roadmap for the rest of the book, and could be adapted by the reader for a specific migration project.

Part II: Software Development Migration

This part provides an implementation basis for the software development migration. It presents details on how to migrate each application element: client and business components code, data, integration and services, logging, monitoring, alerting, and configuration.

For each element, the book provides a clearly defined organizational structure in every chapter: *implementation objectives, when, participants, input, process and activities, outputs and deliverables, tools, techniques, and best practices*, including a critical migration element – resource costs. This structure is preserved throughout the text.

Theory is not worth much without practice, so practical implementation of the migration is supported with design materials, diagrams, sample application code, and cloud configured environments. The objective is to bridge theoretical concepts and practical realizations and assist in real-life migration implementation via running code examples in a physical environment.

Part III: Software Delivery Migration

This part focuses on cloud-agnostic, automated, and secure software delivery. It starts with an agile primer to familiarize readers with definitions of tools-backed implementation checklists and cloud-native pipelines.

In the CICD automaton pipeline sample, there is a wealth of implementation details on various types of testing. In addition to the all-familiar unit, function, integration, and performance testing, the book introduces cloud-critical static application security testing (SAST), dynamic application security testing (DAST), containers compliance and security scanning, and open source dependency testing. It closes with an introduction to chaos engineering to ensure application resiliency in a distributed computing environment.

To understand and control the cloud-migration progress, the book introduces an industry accepted set of DORA metrics—Deployment Frequency (DF), Mean Lead Time for Change (MLT), Mean Time to Recovery (MTTR), and Change Failure Rate (CFR)—to evaluate the migration progress, velocity, and quality.

Part IV: Software Operations Migration

The last part provides directions and implementation details of cost-efficient, automated, policy driven, and cloud-native software operations. It covers and demonstrates realization of important concepts, such as:

- Plan and implement the migration of the production environment, from an on-premise datacenter to a cloud provider infrastructure

- Efficient resource and cost management, implemented via resource tagging, budgeting, and reporting automation

- Cloud-native observability, implemented via automated logging, monitoring, and alerting software stack

- Disaster recovery, implemented via automated failover and restore automated processes

It is vitally important to ensure that the software development and software delivery phases are applied with cost-efficiency as a critical guiding principle. Only then, can you realize cloud-computing benefits and achieve the desired competitive advantage.

Supplementary Terms

There are some terms in the book that require upfront definitions. These terms are introduced and explained in the *Process and Activities, Output and Deliverables, and Shared Responsibility Model* sections.

Process and Activities

The objective of the book is to navigate novice cloud users through conceptual cloud migration with easy-to-follow code examples. To address the vastness of the cloud environment landscape, the following approach has been taken. Some tasks and activities are completed in-full, while others are presented in a simplified form, or are only present as a reference. The expectation is that you can perform these tasks, while the book provides valuable information, pointers, and links to the help materials. To ensure that we convey real-life cloud migration experiences, deep-dive tasks are present and marked to be only implemented as required for an enterprise-grade, production implementation. There is always a note about these tasks that describes what a real-life implementation recommendation would look like.

Outputs and Deliverables

In addition, there will be two types of deliverables related to tasks and activities. Some outputs are implemented to explain the concepts and support a sample project, and marked as *completed here*. The source code for this book is available on GitHub via the book's product page, located at *www.apress.com/9781484272510*.

Other deliverables, derived from real-life migration experience, are included for user reference and enterprise-grade production implementation, and they are marked as *real-life*. The logic behind this classification is straightforward. It allows the author to meet two conflicting goals for the book; keep the text both comprehensive and concise, while guiding the users through a minimum set of technical exercises and providing a pragmatic implementation of these theoretical concepts. In addition, this approach preserves valuable real-life experiences for the users to implement in their environment.

Shared Responsibility Model

The shared responsibility model is another important concept. The outputs and deliverables are marked to be delivered by either the *Product* or the *Platform* team. This classification is somewhat arbitrary and dependent on the organizational structure as well as skillset distribution within the software development teams. If the Product team has a system engineer, any tasks in this area will become the Product team responsibilities, while a typical enterprise will have system engineers separated into their own enterprise infrastructure teams, called Platform teams.

PART I

Introduction to Cloud Computing

Part I of the book introduces the essential cloud computing concepts and builds foundational knowledge on the subject. It establishes a context domain for the rest of the book, for both theoretical and practical concerns.

Chapter 1 dissects an original paper on cloud computing, published by the National Institute of Standards and Technology (NIST) in September of 2011. It is important for the reader to establish a solid understanding of cloud computing, including its characteristics and delivery and service models, as these elements serve as core migration waypoints and influence design and technology decisions. These concepts also influence the practical implementation of the sample application. Next, the reader is presented with cloud computing benefits and drawbacks in three major areas: *business, technology, and social.* The reader is also introduced to paradigm changes in the six major services and technologies knowledge areas: *infrastructure, security, architecture, software development, software delivery, and software operations.* This classification is applied to the rest of the book to structure the migration process.

Chapter 2 starts with organizational cloud migration success factors—*people, processes, and technology*—where successful migration implies deep synergy among all elements. We build on the cloud computing characteristics and its delivery and service models to derive suitable cloud migration architecture and design principles, methodologies, maturity models, technologies, and migration strategies. The chapter ends by presenting the reader with a pragmatic and reusable application cloud migration process that could serve as a blueprint or template for an existing system migration.

CHAPTER 1

Cloud Computing Primer

Cloud-native sits top of mind for everyone, but its success rests on the backs of very few.

—André Christ, LeanIX CEO

This chapter introduces fundamental *cloud computing* concepts, including a short history, to clarify how cloud computing became the next evolutionary step in the information technology. After reading this chapter and studying the materials, you should:

- Have a good understanding of the cloud computing concepts and building blocks; *the essential characteristics, delivery methods, and service models*.

- Recognize cloud computing benefits and drawbacks in *the business, technology, and society areas*.

- Understand cloud-driven paradigm changes in the following technology and services knowledge areas: infrastructure, security, architecture, software development, software delivery, and software operations (Infra, Sec, Arch, Dev, DevSecOps, Ops).

From the beginning of time and through a variety of historical production models humankind has worked tirelessly to become more efficient by inventing tools and designing more effective manufacturing processes. As an example, modern corporations have increased their outputs and reduced costs via economies of scale by combining workers and machinery at a single location to achieve higher efficiency, productivity, and resource utilization rate.

This fundamental production theory and the subsequent results did not go unnoticed, and they have profoundly influenced intellectuals in the computer science and information technology discipline. They paved the way for a variety of

© Taras Gleb 2021
T. Gleb, *Systematic Cloud Migration*, https://doi.org/10.1007/978-1-4842-7252-7_1

concepts and approaches on how to utilize computing resources more efficiently and achieve economies of scale similar to other industries. Early history produced the concept of time-sharing of mainframe machines, and as computers became more widespread, academia and engineers started to explore more ways to offer large-scale computers to a wider user base.

The invention of internet and advances in telecommunication networking, established connectivity, and the concept of resource time-sharing were all results of this effort. Scientists and technologists began experimenting with algorithms that would optimize infrastructure and compute utilization. This evolution eventually manifested itself as a set of services offered by Amazon and was branded as the Amazon Web Services (AWS) family of products.

What Is Cloud Computing?

The fundamental nature of cloud computing can be broadly defined as follows:

> *Cloud computing is a model for enabling ubiquitous, convenient, on-demand network access to a shared pool of configurable computing resources (e.g., networks, servers, storage, applications, and services) that can be rapidly provisioned and released with minimal management effort or service provider interaction.*

> *—Mell and Grance (2011)*

These capabilities are supported by multiple geographically-dispersed datacenters, owned by third-party providers that rely on sharing resources to achieve economies of scale and service coherency. Cloud computing datacenters typically operate high-capacity networks for service delivery from low-cost and hardware-virtualized network, compute, and storage devices.

According to Mell and Grance (2011), the original cloud computing model is composed of five essential characteristics, four delivery models, and three service models (see Figure 1-1).

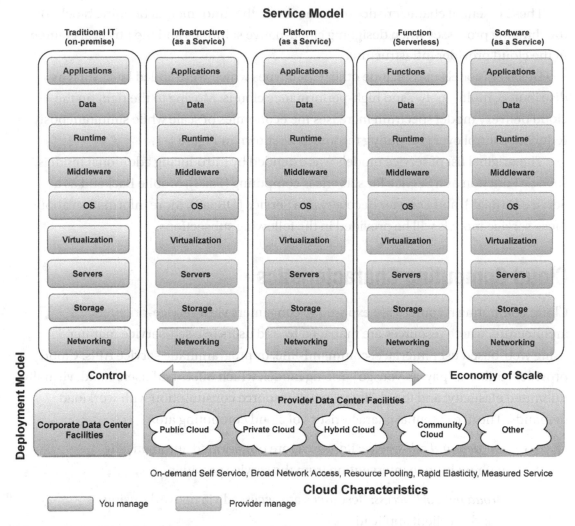

Figure 1-1. *The cloud computing model*

- *Five essential characteristics:* On-demand self-service, broad network access, resource pooling, rapid elasticity, and measured service

- *Four delivery models:* Private cloud, community cloud, public cloud, and hybrid cloud

- *Three service models:* Infrastructure as a Service (IaaS), Platform as a Service (PaaS), and Software as a Service (SaaS)

These essential characteristics represent both, the fundamental building blocks of the thinking processes when designing cloud-native solutions and the physical elements in the cloud provider infrastructure.

Delivery models may include other cloud types which were added later, such as distributed, multi-, poly-, and high-performance clouds. Moving to the right on the cloud delivery model spectrum increases the economies of scale while simultaneously reducing control over computing resources, as shown in Figure 1-1.

The original list of service models was extended by introducing additional models, such as Function as a Service for serverless computing (FaaS), Mobile Backend as a Service (MBaaS), and Disaster Recovery as a Service (DRaaS). More information about these service models will be provided in the following subsections.

Cloud Computing Characteristics

Cloud computing resources are exposed to consumers via a service-oriented architecture, where resources are managed by end users in a self-service manner, using web-based user interface, command-line, or programmatic service APIs. Cloud providers utilize a "pay-as-you-go" pricing model, which offers end users rapid, virtually unlimited elasticity, and the ability to match resource consumption with workload demands. The five essential characteristics of cloud computing are:

- *On-demand self-service:* Resources are provisioned automatically without human intervention from the service provider.

- *Broad network access:* Resources are accessed via networks using standard client applications.

- *Resource pooling:* Resources are pooled and shared among multiple customers using the multi-tenant model.

- *Rapid elasticity:* Resources are elastically provisioned and scaled up and down as needed.

- *Measured service:* The provider automatically measures, controls, and optimizes resource usage.

The Cloud Deployment Model

Cloud computing resources could be shared between various tenants or dedicated to a single customer. They can also be combined in various manners, which depends on the cloud provider's capability and the software's functional and non-functional requirements. Based on the presented criteria, the following *deployment models* are available:

- *Public:* Resources operated by the public cloud provider are shared and available to multiple organizations or tenants and delivered over public internet or private, direct connections.

- *Private:* Resources are managed by the private cloud provider; they are not shared and only consumed within the operating organization.

- *Hybrid:* Offers a combination of resources and related deployments, both within public cloud and on-premise datacenters.

- *Community:* Resources and cloud infrastructure are typically shared between several organizations that are part of a specific community (compliance, geography, jurisdiction, security, etc.).

- *Distributed:* Cloud computing resources are brought together from a dispersed set of machines in different geographical locations, connected to a single hub or network service. It could be a public-resource computing cloud or a volunteer cloud.

- *Multi-cloud:* A combination of multiple clouds computing into a heterogeneous cloud architecture to eliminate dependence on a single vendor, cloud type, or location.

- *Poly-cloud:* A combination of multiple cloud providers, similar to multi-cloud, but the objective is to enhance cloud offerings by joining services from various providers and achieve synergy.

- *High performing computing (HPC):* Cloud computing and infrastructure for high-performance applications.

Despite the proliferation of these cloud-deployment models, the majority of the solutions deployed by IT teams fall under three models: public, private, and hybrid clouds.

The Cloud Services Model

The cloud computing service delivery model started with three basic service delivery models:

- *Infrastructure as a Service (IaaS):* Compute, networking, and OS are supplied on-demand and billed on a utility computing basis, without need to operate, manage, or control the infrastructure. Users install OS images and applications on the provider's infrastructure, and are responsible for OS maintenance, patching, and security updates. The provider is responsible for the physical datacenter, virtual machines, and networking. Examples of IaaS include AWS EC2 and Azure VMs. IaaS services in the organization are typically the responsibility of the infrastructure and network platform teams.

- *Platform as a Service (PaaS):* Represents a pre-defined development environment, an OS, a database-as-a-service, a web server, a runtime environment, an integrated middleware-as-a-service, or a suite of pre-built tools to support a full development lifecycle. Providers operate, manage, and perform OS patching, security updates, software maintenance, data backup and replications, and compute and storage resource scalability. Development teams do not need to manually allocate infrastructure, as in the previous model, but can instead focus on building, testing, and deploying business applications. This model lets development teams achieve higher productivity by relegating lower-value administration tasks to the cloud provider. PaaS services are billed on a per-service basis, either per service hour or some other kind of service metric (GB of database storage). Newer variations of PaaS include Function as a Service (FaaS) and Mobile Backend as a Service (MBaaS). Examples of PaaS include Google App Engine, AWS Elastic Beanstalk, Heroku, and Google Firebase. PaaS services in the organization are typically consumed by the application development's Product teams.

- Software as a Service (SaaS): Users have access to business software, while the cloud and service providers manage the software, as well as the underlying infrastructure and platforms (including application and user data). SaaS services are typically subscription-based with flat monthly or annual per user fees. Users do not need to install applications on their devices. Instead, applications are accessed via the Web UI or API endpoints. Examples of SaaS include Gmail, Trello, and Office 365. PaaS services in the organization are typically consumed by end users.

The most recent concept of *everything as a service (XaaS)* has led to the emergence of multiple services in different areas (e.g., Mobile Backend as a Service (MBaaS), Disaster Recovery as a Service (DRaaS), the list goes on). Upon closer look, these services simply represent variations of *PaaS* solutions. Each delivery model progressively abstracts a particular hardware or software layer in the following stack: infrastructure, platform, or software applications. All service models introduce clearly defined responsibility models, where we match responsibility or usage of the layer to the end user, the product team, or the platform team.

Cloud Advantages and Drawbacks

Cloud computing has advantages and challenges to be aware of, so you can ensure that your cloud migration is effective, cost efficient, and overall beneficial to your organization. The classification of pros and cons in this section focuses on three major areas: *business, technology, and society*. Advantages and drawbacks of each area are further broken down into the related subsections.

Business

Business organizations have already undergone tremendous transformations brought about by the Internet and globalization. Cloud computing added another set of variables or dimensions to the equation. If implemented correctly, cloud computing may bring both, many potential advantages, as well as challenges, to the business organization.

Advantages:

- Focus limited IT resources on core competencies to enhance firm competitive advantage.

- Utilize new services and products to deliver value, services, and products faster, and anywhere in the world to support globalization and new market development.

- Provision infrastructure and software applications into the geography of choice to support compliance, agility, velocity, and data locality requirements.

- Reduce software and hardware administration and infrastructure costs by using the cloud provider's data center hardware and software services.

- Replace capital investment with operational leasing costs. There's no longer need for upfront capital investment into hardware or software for projects implementation.

- Increase productivity, release organization resources from non-value added activities via utilization of cloud provider offerings, as well as relegate manual administrative tasks to cloud services.

- Promote learning, and innovation within an organization through the cloud providers' services, such as AI and ML, out of the box.

- Reduce or mitigate a project's technology and financial implementation risks.

- Increase collaboration between globally dispersed organizational resources.

Drawbacks:

- Substantial investment required to adapt the new technologies, both in terms of solution implementation and personnel training.

- Cost overruns due to inefficiencies in cloud migration implementation and operation.

- SaaS delivery model places the organizational data in the cloud provider's custody. This increases security risks of unauthorized access, should there be a breach in the cloud provider's security environment.

- Application deployments and data flows may expose the organization business model to the competitors and the cloud provider.

- Vendor lock-in could affect an organization's bottom line and its ability to switch providers if prices providers charge for their services increase.

Technology

Where cloud shines the most, is in the technology area. So far cloud computing has delivered substantial benefits to different sectors, including information technology itself, financial, automotive, and pharmaceuticals; the list goes on. Technology advantages and drawbacks include the following, see the list below.

Advantages:

- Cloud provider's datacenters provide hardware and software redundancy and high-availability.

- Virtually unlimited, automated, on-demand dynamic elasticity, as well as hardware and software scalability, to match workloads to resource requirements and avoid over-provisioning and waste.

- Shared responsibility security model eliminates gaps in hardware and software security configurations.

- Ability to avoid single point of failure in the technology stack.

- Automatic hardware and software updates.

- Automated disaster recovery implementation in any geographical region to satisfy data locality requirements.

- Benefit from cloud provider's software and hardware innovations.

Drawbacks:

- Distributed environment of the cloud computing introduces development, implementation, and maintenance complexity into the software systems.

- Retraining IT staff or hiring new resources that have cloud-related skills and abilities.

- Reduced control over hardware and software stack. Dependency on the outsourced cloud provider's technical support.

- Shared pool of resources may lead to resource shortage if demand outpaces the ability of the cloud provider to bring new datacenters online.

- Inadequate compliance and regulatory implementation for edge cases.

11

Social

Although the impact of cloud computing on the business and technology areas is widely understood and accepted, cloud influence on society and environment is generally less visible or debated. Advantages and drawbacks include the following.

Advantages:

- Sustainability. Cloud providers have committed to reduction of environmental impact (e.g., Google's policy is to ensure that all datacenters are 100% carbon neutral).

- Cloud computing has created new business and learning capabilities around the globe to reduce poverty and promote new business opportunities.

Drawbacks:

- Consumer data collection and analysis without consent or understanding the usage patterns. This leads to ethical and privacy concerns of data location, sale, and exposure.

- Digital divide. A social and economic split could emerge as a result of limited access to cloud computing, learning opportunities, or earning potential.

- Uneven playing field. Uneven access to cloud computing resources may lead to creation of more monopolistic, dictatorial, or oligopolistic societies.

Cloud Paradigm Shifts

Any introduction to cloud computing would be incomplete without highlighting the fundamental paradigm changes that we must be aware of. These shifts are to be clearly understood in order to successfully complete application migration. New technologies are often being implemented with old paradigms in mind. This mismatch leads to situations where, instead of getting promised benefits, teams end up fighting and struggling with new technologies, introducing anti-patterns, additional complexity, and technical debt.

This book groups those paradigm changes into six distinct technology and services areas (with abbreviations). These are also our migration focus areas: Architecture (Arch), Software Development (Dev), Software Delivery (DevSecOps), Software Operations (Ops), Security (Sec), and Infrastructure (Infra), as depicted in Figure 1-2.

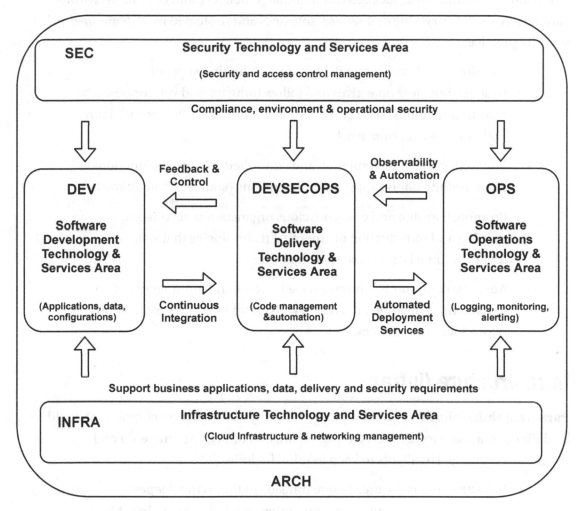

Figure 1-2. *Cloud migration technology and services areas*

Architecture (Arch)

Paradigm shift: cloud-native and evolutionary architecture (sources ThoughtWorks and Google) that designs stateless software, built with cloud-native, cost-efficient and open-source technologies, packaged for automated delivery and operations within various flavors of *'everything as a service'* software, and protected by *'defense-in-depth'* security practice.

- Develop cloud-native architecture principles that support strategic business objectives and follow industry and vendor best recommendations, such as *AWS Well-Architectured Pillars* and *Azure Well Architected Framework.*

- Maintain guided, incremental, and controlled (via fitness functions) change along important system dimensions (source: ThoughtWorks).

- Promote learning and cost-conscious organization via ongoing training and introduction of emerging technologies that sustain organizational IT and business objectives.

- Advance continuous innovation via incremental improvements, derived from ongoing integration with cloud provider's innovations in products and services.

Infrastructure (Infra)

Paradigm shift: Infrastructure as a code, where any infrastructure component could be defined as a software, delivered on-demand, as a utility, with metered and usage-based billing. Highlights to keep in mind include:

- Infrastructure is the area where transformation is the deepest, and it influences, determines, and drives related changes in other technology and services areas. Virtualized vs. physical hardware provides geolocation independence, enables provisioning elasticity to match workloads and resources, takes advantage of cost reduction, and eliminates the problem of hardware over-provisioning.

- Customers benefit from the latest cloud provider hardware innovations, which instantly become available once they are released in the datacenters. Application code and supporting infrastructure can match and evolve in tandem, which was previously unheard of.

- Developers can provision infrastructure in a self-service manner, reducing, or in some cases eliminating, the need for infrastructure and network administrators. High-availability, self-healing, resiliency, automatic failover, and redundancy are provided out-of-the-box for critical infrastructure and networking components. Infrastructure code definitions could be stored in the code repository for automation and repeatability.

- Introduction of containerization technology, as an evolutionary hardware virtualization approach, to further enhance software density and utilization of computational hardware resources.

Security (Sec)

Paradigm shift: Introduction of the shared responsibility model, where the customer, the service, and the cloud provider all participate in protecting the data, the applications, the network, and the infrastructure. Highlights to keep in mind include:

- *Everything as a Code (XaaC),* where security configurations are implemented via code-driven policies, stored in the code repository, and verified for compliance, performance, and capacity.

- Machine Learning (ML) and Artificial Intelligence (AI), where security capabilities allow for automatic threat prediction, detection, alerting, and mitigation.

- The shared responsibility model, where customers leverage cloud-provider security capabilities and eliminate any gaps that might exist in the on-premise datacenters. Cloud provider security services considerably improve detection and response time, as depicted in Figure 1-3.

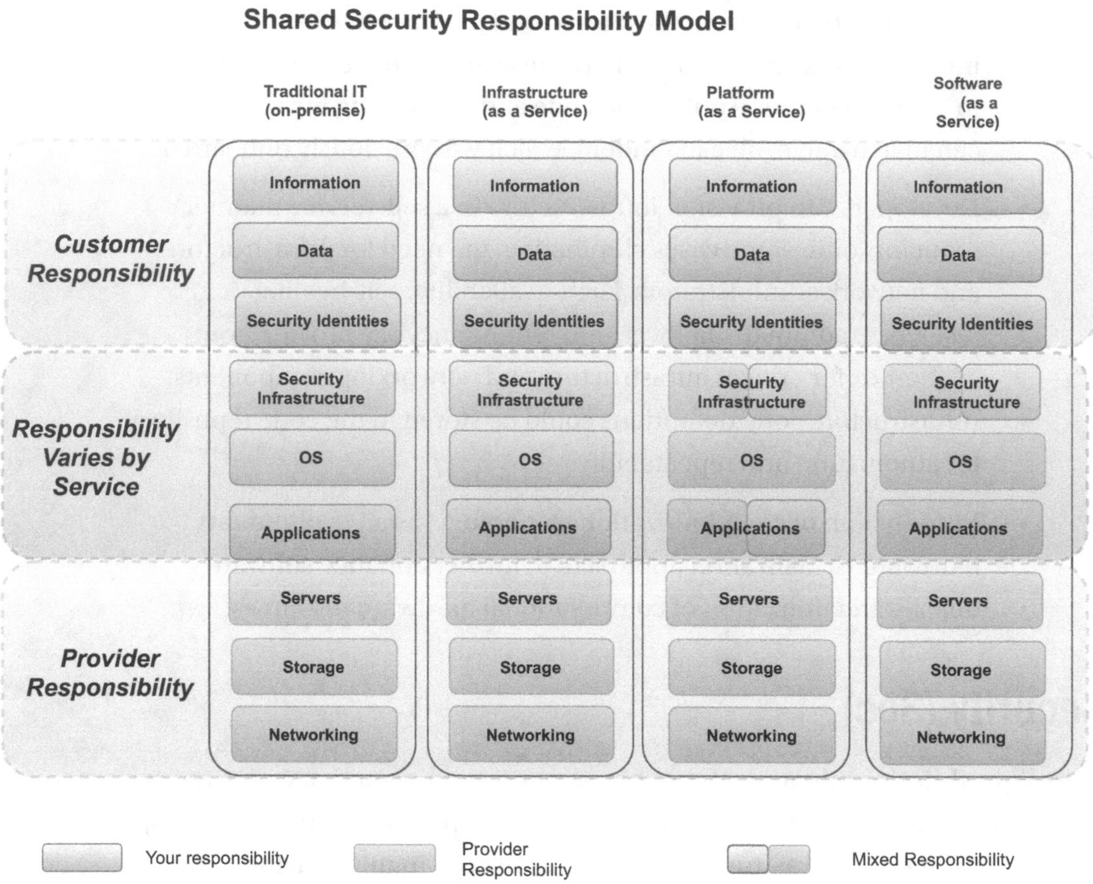

Shared Security Responsibility Model

	Traditional IT (on-premise)	Infrastructure (as a Service)	Platform (as a Service)	Software (as a Service)
Customer Responsibility	Information	Information	Information	Information
	Data	Data	Data	Data
	Security Identities	Security Identities	Security Identities	Security Identities
Responsibility Varies by Service	Security Infrastructure	Security Infrastructure	Security Infrastructure	Security Infrastructure
	OS	OS	OS	OS
	Applications	Applications	Applications	Applications
Provider Responsibility	Servers	Servers	Servers	Servers
	Storage	Storage	Storage	Storage
	Networking	Networking	Networking	Networking

Your responsibility   Provider Responsibility   Mixed Responsibility

Figure 1-3. *The shared security responsibility model*

Software Development (Dev)

Paradigm shift: Reduced or eliminated dependency on infrastructure teams. The cloud provider services and automates software to achieve unconstrained agility and velocity in software application development and delivery. Highlights to keep in mind include:

- Introduction of Docker containers allows business applications to run in containers and eliminate the need for virtual machine-level administration. In addition, containerization provides elastic up-and down-scaling to match load and provisioned resource requirements.

- Container orchestration and packaging software provides for declarative vs. imperative deployment configurations for efficient, repetitive, idempotent deployment, upgrade, and rollback.

- Applications consume common services in the cloud as a code or API endpoint. Examples include infrastructure, data, security, logging, monitoring, and alerting.

Software Delivery (DevSecOps)

Paradigm shift: A cloud-native approach to software release and process automation. It promotes and supports the agile software delivery lifecycle methodology to deliver application, infrastructure, and security as a code. Highlights to keep in mind include:

- Introduction of *GitOps* principles and *DevSecOps* practices allow for automated, high-velocity software delivery without compromising security, quality, or compliance. Consistency and correctness has increased significantly with everything under version control.

- Reduction in bureaucracy within the software delivery process through clearly traceable collaboration and ownership. This is done by applying the DevSecOps methodology and its software tools.

- Integrated cloud-first development and delivery process maximizes the time invested in IT personnel, because teams can spend their time on value-added activities while buying commodity services.

- Declarative over imperative software deployment approach. We describe the target system state, either infrastructure or application, and the software automatically monitors the actual state and corrects deviations to return the system to the target state.

Software Operations (Ops)

Paradigm shift: Rapid, elastic, and metered resource provisioning to match the workload for cost-efficiency. Includes comprehensive observability, automation, and alerting that are uniform across all the virtually-defined hardware and software stacks. Highlights to keep in mind include:

- Reduce or eliminate over-provisioning of hardware resources for runtime environments. Automated elasticity to match software workload requirements with service provider compute, storage, and networking resources.

- Teams can leverage the cloud provider infrastructure for collection, storage, and back-up of the monitoring data and enable services for insights, advanced analysis, as well as enhances searching and investigation capabilities. Oftentimes, availability of AI and ML augmented security information and event management for threat detection and response.

Summary

This chapter explained the formal definitions for cloud computing, its fundamental characteristics, and the available deployment and services models. Benefits include *on-demand self-service, broad network access, resource pooling, rapid elasticity, and measured services*. These benefits are the cornerstones to designing and implementing solutions in cloud provider environments.

This chapter discussed the benefits and pitfalls of cloud computing in the *business, technology, and social* areas. The goal is to ensure that the migration process takes these issues into consideration and is effective and cost efficient, while bringing business value and competitive advantage to the organization.

Last, but not least, this chapter explained the fundamental paradigm changes in six important technology and service migration areas: *infrastructure, security, software development, software delivery, and software operations*. Utilizing these new paradigms will ensure that the cloud-native thinking process is applied during the migration design and implementation processes. That thinking process should be consistent with cloud computing *characteristics, deployment, and delivery models*.

CHAPTER 2

Cloud Migration Fundamentals

Life requires all the pieces, not just the ones that we tend to like.

— Craig D. Lounsbrough

Chapter 1 presented an in-depth introduction to cloud computing, including its essential characteristics, service delivery models, and deployment models. This chapter continues to build on those concepts and includes the following objectives:

- Establish essential organizational capabilities in the core areas of *people, process, and technologies*, consistent with cloud computing characteristics to support effective and efficient cloud migration.

- Present and understand migration strategies, design principles, maturity models, and cloud-native technologies that represent architecture and software development migration building blocks.

This chapter wraps up with a step-by-step, hands-on process that depicts migration implementation for the sample Java based web application. The generic process presented in this chapter could serve as an abstracted template or blueprint for any migration project regardless of technology stack, programming language, or cloud provider.

It is reasonable to assume that effective cloud migration depends on more than one element and, as such, we believe could be centered on the three major factors as shown in Figure 2-1.

- *Organizational structure, also known as people migration factors:* Focused on product and platform teams, shared responsibility model, cloud-native approach to problem solving, and cultural transformation to build cost-efficient, learning, and innovative organizations.

19

© Taras Gleb 2021
T. Gleb, *Systematic Cloud Migration*, https://doi.org/10.1007/978-1-4842-7252-7_2

- *Migration frameworks, tools and software or technology migration factors:* Take into consideration cloud-native design principles, maturity models, software products, best practices, tools and techniques.

- *Cloud migration process or process migration factors:* Focus on comprehensive, detailed, and pragmatic cloud migration processes.

Warning   Do not attempt to change all three classes simultaneously, as organizations and teams need sensible balance between change rate and stability.

To migrate effectively and efficiently, you need to understand that migration success is determined by the synergies between these three factors. Given the Conway's Law impact on software development, people, processes, and technologies factors have all to be aligned to both reduce friction between those elements and enable synergy.

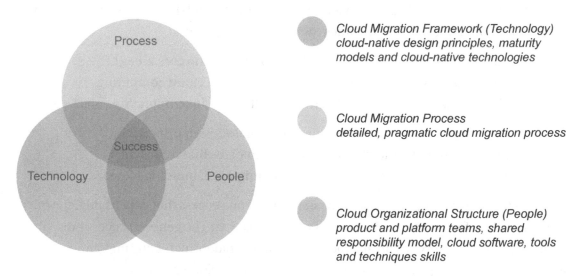

Figure 2-1. *Cloud migration success factors*

You also need to make certain that there is a healthy balance between change rate and stability within and between each factor. In addition, when you attempt to introduce a new software development process, methodology, or technology, you have to evaluate its impact on factors in other areas.

Cloud Organizational Structure (People)

The software development process is strongly affected by the organizational structure, culture, communication patterns, and style. This phenomenon has been observed and formulated by Conway's Law, which states:

> *Any organization that designs a system (defined broadly) will produce a design whose structure is a copy of the organization's communication structure.*
>
> — *Melvin E. Conway (1968)*

With this in mind, we need to consider how we organize information technology teams, what types of teams we have in place, the teams' responsibilities, and required skillsets. Based on the earlier definition of *six migration technology and services areas,* this book recommends two main types of teams—a *Product Team and a Platform Team*:

- *Product Team*: A self-sufficient, self-organized, and self-managed team responsible for building, deploying, and operating business software applications. This team consists of software developers, architects, quality assurance specialists, database administrators, operations engineers, and DevSecOps engineers. They have the sufficient skillset to be responsible for executing full software development lifecycle functions. The team's software product will consume services offered by the cloud provider, third parties, as well as the Platform team.

- *Platform Team*: A self-sufficient, self-organized, and self-managed team that builds, deploys, and operates platform-type services, such as infrastructure, networking, security, and enterprise productivity services. This team will also consume the cloud provider's and third-party services, while providing their Software as a Service (e.g., IaaS) to the Product team.

This type of organizational IT structure provides sufficient specialization and flexibility to support agile migration processes. It clearly defines and separates the teams' responsibilities and technology areas and allows teams to move independently of each other.

Cloud Migration Framework (Technologies)

The next important element is the *cloud migration framework*—encapsulation of a clear, concise, and comprehensive set of guiding principles, design models, industry practices, resources, and technologies that describe how a team makes critical decisions in selecting a migration strategy, a maturity model, a technology, or a process. The framework's application to the solution design, results in a resilient, secure, high-performing, and cost-efficient solution that adheres to the cloud migration soundness pillars described below:

- *Cloud-native technology:* Delivering scalable, resilient, and efficient software applications that can be run in public, private, or hybrid clouds.

- *Operational excellence:* Running cloud-native applications that continually improve quality of software operations while delivering business value.

- *Cost optimization*: Introducing cost as a design criteria and iteratively reducing cloud-related operational costs while providing quality of service, security, performance. and reliability.

- *Quality, performance, and reliability*: Making sure the application performs all intended business functions to support quality and business level requirements.

- *Security:* Protecting system components and information, ensuring data confidentiality and integrity, with ability to detect security events and provide timely response and mitigation.

Cloud Migration Design Principles

Design principles applied and introduced in technology and services areas are not entirely new. They existed before cloud computing became mainstream and have been adopted and modified to better fit cloud computing models. It is worth noting that this list is not absolute; each particular migration scenario may call for additional industry, technology, or business-related principles. The list below presents industry accepted cloud-native or cloud-friendly design principles, grouped by technology and service area:

- Software Application Development Area (Dev)

  - *Twelve factors app methodology* (`https://12factor.net/`): Supportive of the software-as-a-service concept and extremely suitable for the cloud computing model.

  - *Cloud maturity model*: Concerned with selecting the appropriate deployment and delivery model for the application, data, integration, and services, as per Mell and Grance (2011) research on cloud computing.

  - *Cloud-agnostic solution:* Chooses design that uses cloud-native technologies while simultaneously applying a suitable risk-mitigating, vendor-agnostic approach.

  - *Cloud computing characteristics:* Applies a self-healing, self-service, automation centric, cost-efficient approach to solution design.

  - *Cloud open-source software*: Chooses open-source, cloud-native technologies, frameworks, and programming tools as recommended by industry standards and organizations such as CNCF.

- Software Delivery Area (DevSecOps)

  - Even though there are numerous DevOps principles that support cloud-native software delivery, they all focus, to a different degree, on automating, collaborating, and promoting *everything-as-a-code* (XaaC) approach and integrating services from various areas through software-based processes:

    - *DevOps (Dev-to-Ops):* Describes a set of activities that combine software development (Dev) and IT operations (Ops).

    - *GitOps (Dev-to-Infra):* Introduces practices that combine deployment with infrastructure and observability.

- *DevSecOps (Dev-to-Sec-to-Ops)*: Integrates security practices into DevOps.

- *AIOps, DataOps, MLOps:* The natural evolution of DevOps practices for a particular area of IT, such as artificial intelligence, data management, and machine learning management.

- *Teams shared responsibility mode:* Focuses on separation of concerns and duties between Platform and Product teams.

- Software Operations (Ops)

  - *Site reliability engineering (https://sre.google/)*: Discipline invented by Google that blends software engineering and operations, where main objective is to create cloud-native, highly-reliable, observable, and scalable systems.

  - *Operational efficiency:* Looks into cost-conscious teams that apply cost as design, implementation, and operations criteria as opposed to a post-implementation optimization factor.

- Infrastructure Technology and Services Area (Infra)

  - *Infrastructure as a Service*: An approach to infrastructure automation that stresses consistent and repeatable processes for provisioning and managing infrastructure systems.

- Security Technology and Services Area (Sec)

  - *Security as a Service (SecaaS):* Similar to IaaS, provides automation, consistency, and high-reliability for system protection in the cloud environment.

  - *Security shared responsibility model:* Cloud security framework that dictates separating security responsibilities between the cloud provider and the end user.

  - *Zero Trust security mode:* Network security model based on strict identity verification processes.

  - *Defense in depth:* Security defense strategy that accepts the fact that breach is possible and relies on multiple lines of defense.

- Architecture Area (Arch)

  - *Evolutionary architecture:* Supports guided, incremental, and controlled (via fitness functions) change along important system dimensions (source: ThoughtWorks).

  - *Cloud-native architecture:* Designed for automation, stateless managed services, cloud-native and open-source technologies, and practices defense-in-depth security.

  - *Cloud-native architecture principles:* Follows industry and vendors' best practices and architecture principles, such as AWS well-architectured pillars and Azure well architected framework.

  - *Build a cost-conscious organization:* Integrates solution cost discussions into organizational culture, solution architecture and design process as opposed to being an optimization afterthought.

  - *Promote a learning organization:* Achieves continuous innovation via incremental improvements from ongoing training, learning, and cloud provider's innovations.

Maturity Models

The cloud maturity model is directly impacted by NIST characteristics of cloud computing (*on-demand self-service, broad network access, resource pooling, rapid elasticity, measured service*), as well as definitions of service models (*IaaS, PaaS, and SaaS*), with more emphasis on service models. We can, to a certain degree, disregard delivery models in our evaluation (*private, community, public, and hybrid cloud*), as they have limited impact on application architecture, code, and deployment approach. We can then classify workloads to be *cloud-ready, cloud-friendly, cloud-resilient, or cloud-native*, given how they relate to architecture, design, and deployment approach (see Table 2-1) This taxonomy is based on the Pivotal Software workload classification (see *www.youtube.com/watch?v=cpgsz4omUOA&t=1649s*).

Table 2-1. *Cloud Workload Maturity Classification*

Cloud-native	Microservices architecture
	API first design
Cloud-resilient	Fault-tolerant and resilient design
	Cloud-agnostic runtime integration
	Bundled metrics and monitoring
	Proactive failure testing
Cloud-friendly	12-factor application methodology
	Horizontally scalable
	Leverage platform for high availability
Cloud-ready	No permanent disk access
	Self-contained application
	Platform-managed ports and networking
	Consumes platform managed backing services

Workload classification is superimposed over the NIST service model to identify where each workload classification lands. The results are not precise, as there is a substantial amount of variability in the workloads architecture and design, as well as how they land into the cloud services. However, it clearly demonstrates the trend, which indicates that moving to the right on the service model spectrum provides us with the greater degree of cloud maturity (see Figure 2-2).

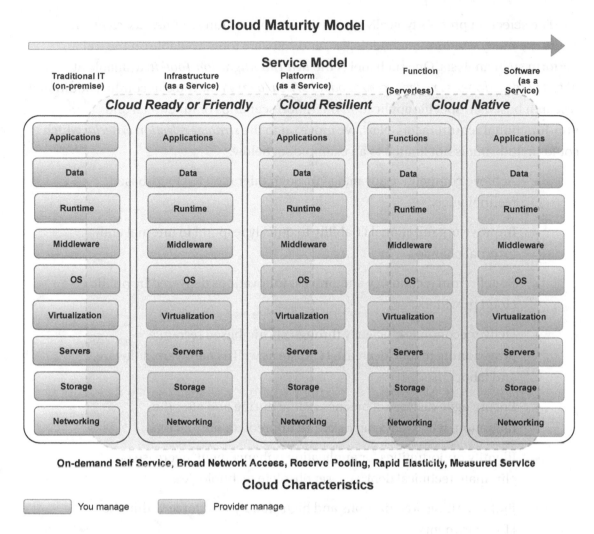

Figure 2-2. *Cloud maturity model*

Migration Strategies

The cloud migration strategy selection is a complex and multi-step process. It depends on a large number of factors and requires input from a diverse set of stakeholders within and outside of the organization. We should also take into consideration the internal and external organizational environmental factors. On one side of the complexity spectrum we might have monolithic or even mainframe applications, while the other side is represented by virtualized, service-oriented or micro-services applications.

The selection process typically starts with an application *readiness assessment*. There are many vendors, methodologies, and software tools available on the web to perform such analysis. One such tool is the *Red Hat Migration Toolkit*, available at `https://developers.redhat.com/products/mta/overview`. You can conduct additional research based on specific application migration scenarios or functional and non-functional requirements. Next, we move on to the *strategy selection criteria*, which could include but is not limited to an example set below:

- Achieve competitive advantage through migration to cloud-based technologies.

- Improve organizational IT ability to quickly respond to internal and external changes.

- Benefit from technology and process innovations delivered by public cloud providers.

- Deliver economic efficiency through elastic-based resource provisioning model, decrease IT waste as well as hardware, software, and labor costs.

- Ensure agile delivery of business value during and after the migration, while reducing risks and unpredictability factors.

- Identify opportunities for application enhancement, decrease or eliminate technical debt, sun-set obsolete technologies.

- Build learning organizations and high-quality workforce within the IT departments.

This text presents six common application migration strategies. Table 2-2 provides a description of each strategy, including the evaluation criteria—Migration Effort (Low, Medium, High), Optimization Opportunity (Low, Medium, High), and mapping to the Cloud Delivery Model (Mell and Grance, 2011) and the Cloud Maturity Model. As you move down the table, effort, complexity, benefits, and degree of cloud maturity increases.

Table 2-2. *Cloud Migration Strategy Table*

Migration Strategy	Migration Effort	Optimization Opportunity	Cloud Delivery Model	Cloud Maturity Model
Retire Sunset end-of-life application, technology, or component	Low	Low	N/A	N/A
Retain	Low	Low	IaaS	Cloud-ready
Rehost (Lift &Shift) Allow migrating application quickly with minimal modifications.	Low to Medium	Low to Medium	IaaS, PaaS	Cloud-ready
Repurchase Replace by commercial-off-the-shelf (COTS) or SaaS	Low to Medium	Low to Medium	IaaS, PaaS, SaaS	Cloud-ready Cloud-friendly Cloud-native
Replatform (Lift & Reshape) Change underlying platform, runtime, middleware, framework, package into container	Medium to High	Medium to High	IaaS, PaaS, SaaS	Cloud-ready Cloud-friendly Cloud-native
Refactor (Rebuild) Extend, rewrite, and redesign to take full advantage of the new platform. Business need to add new features or scale.	High	High	IaaS, PaaS, SaaS	Cloud-native

Technologies

It is practically impossible to describe or even list all cloud-native technologies that have emerged within the last few years. AWS, for example, provides thousands of different services and that number continues to grow weekly. What is possible though, is to identify selection criteria, foundational cloud-native technology organizations, and industry standards that promote, support, and help develop cloud-native and open-source solutions.

One such organization, the Cloud Native Computing Foundation (CNCF; *www.cncf.io/*), serves as home to many open-source, cloud-native software project. These projects are developed with NIST defined cloud characteristics in mind, and are suited to run in the cloud provider's environments, deliver high-efficiency, low cost, and high-adaptability. These technologies are designed and built to run in the distributed cloud environment from the very beginning. To provide additional help with cloud technology selection, the following criteria could be applied (see Table 2-3):

Cloud Maturity = Cloud-Ready-1, Cloud-Friendly-3, Cloud-Resilient-4, Cloud-Native-5

Importance = High - 5, Medium - 2, Low – 1

Table 2-3. *Cloud Migration Technology Selection*

Category	Criterion	Cloud Maturity (1 – 5)	Importance (1 – 5)
Business strategy	• Meets current business requirements • Aligned with enterprise, business, and architecture strategy • Able to deliver within program timeline and budget		
Cloud-native maturity model	• Available as a service in the public cloud provider • Available in the regions you are deploying your applications into • Advantages in cost and operational efficiency as compared to self-built solutions • Technology is offered as part of existing cloud-native industry standards body, e.g., CNCF		
Complexity	• Easy to operate • Easy to maintain • Easy to modify • Easy to understand		

(continued)

Table 2-3. (*continued*)

Category	Criterion	Cloud Maturity (1 – 5)	Importance (1 – 5)
Effort	• Development cost • Support and operational cost • Compatibility with existing systems • Reuse of existing system capabilities		
Extensibility	• Reusable, modular, and provides good separation of concerns and loose coupling • Future extensibility is easy • Flexibility, insulate business from impact of IT changes • Supports industry standards and future trends • Utilizes and adheres to industry best practices, standards, and architectural patterns		
Good technology fit	• Easy to integrate and operate within existing technology ecosystem • Supported by the skillset within Product and Platform teams		
Vendor and technology risk mitigation	• Avoids vendor lock-in • Utilize industry standards, formats, and protocols • Commercial open-source solutions are available		
Learning and innovations opportunities	• Supports future technologies, such as Machine Learning and Artificial Intelligence		

The cloud migration technology selection process concludes the cloud migration framework. Having previously established a proper cloud organizational structure, we are now ready to dive into the cloud migration process.

Cloud Migration Process

Cloud migration is the process of moving application components, data, system integrations, and configurations to the cloud provider's environment. The objectives of the process are to:

- Achieve migration objectives effectively and efficiently. Or in simple terms, ensure we are doing the "right thing" (effectiveness) and "doing them right"(efficiency).

- Apply best practices, sound architecture, and recommended tools and techniques.

- Reduce implementation time and cost and avoid cost runaways.

- Identify and mitigate technological and financial migration risks early in the implementation process.

The cloud migration process combines a static view of the migration domain, which consists of technology and service areas presented in the previous chapter (i.e., Arch, Dev, Sec, DevSecOps, Ops, and Infra) with a dynamic process view that identifies the migration steps. In addition, the process maps steps to technology and service areas, and groups them into three logical phases—plan, migrate, and operate. This approach also makes it straightforward to link the migration process to formal project management areas, as depicted in Figure 2-3.

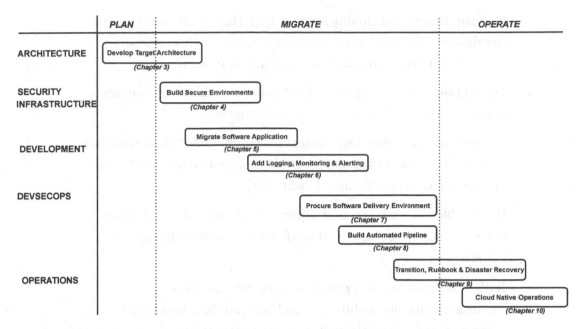

Figure 2-3. *Cloud migration process*

At the end of each step, we deliver tangible results in the form of architecture and software artifacts or provisioned environments (e.g., a Java Spring Boot application packaged in the Docker container and deployed to the Kubernetes cluster). In addition, every step has an identical structure that is easily recognizable to readers familiar with project management methodology (PMO) or software delivery lifecycle (SDLC) frameworks. That structure consists of the following:

- *Objectives*: Describes target deliverables in broader terms (e.g., "Kubernetes cluster exists, is configured, and is ready for application components deployments").

- *When*: Identifies where the step is in the migration process, and if there are any prerequisite steps to be completed.

- *Roles*: Describes a set of roles and skills required to complete the step. Roles include: Developer (Dev, Product Team), Architect (Arch, Product Team), Network Engineer (NetEng, Platform Team), Infrastructure Engineer (InfraEng, Platform Team), Operations Engineer (OpsEng Product Team), Security Engineer (SecEng,

Platform Team), and Quality Analyst (QA). Having roles and teams clearly identified helps establish lines of responsibility and isolation between software components or steps in the process.

- *Inputs*: Lists required inputs of the step (e.g., business requirements documents or architecture components diagram).

- *Processes and activities*: Depicts technical implementation steps that would achieve objectives and the desired output. In the context of this book, it could be "create a Docker file".

- *Deliverables:* Describes actual software or documentation artifacts to be produced (e.g., "application's Docker container deployed to Kubernetes cluster").

- *Tools techniques and best practices*: Lists and describes recommended tools, techniques, and best practices to achieve objectives and build high-quality, cloud-native solutions.

Summary

At this point, you should have a profound understanding of cloud computing, including its *characteristics, delivery and service models*, as well as the related *paradigm changes*. Additionally, you have learned about its effects on *technology, business,* and *society*. Figure 2-4 illustrates all the major fundamental concepts presented up to now and their relationships.

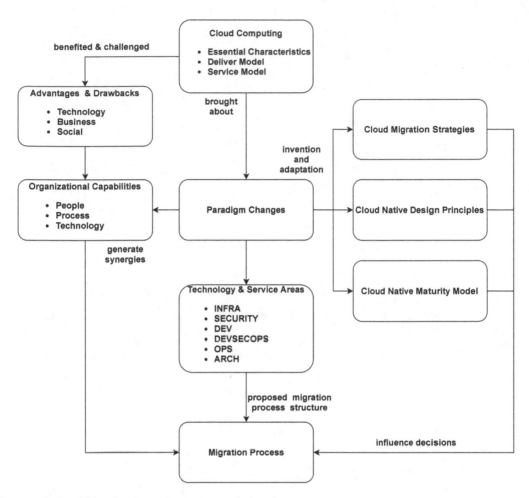

Figure 2-4. *Cloud migration concepts map*

You established *technology and services areas* as well as critical *organizational capabilities* to support the migration. You got familiar with *cloud-native design principles, maturity models, and migration strategies.*

You are now ready to dive into the hands-on migration implementation, using the sample application. The source code for this book is available on GitHub via the book's product page, located at *www.apress.com/9781484272510*. The sample implementation project and related migration model represents a simplified view of these real-world migration scenarios. This approach is designed to help you face real-world scenarios. The idea is to use a simplified model to plainly identify the important parts and steps, while keeping the noise out.

The next step is to plan cloud migration and design future-state architecture.

PART II

Software Development Migration

In this part of the book, you begin the actual, hands-on application migration. All the chapters provide architecture and design deep-dives as well as practical implementation steps within the software development (Dev), technology, and services areas, as depicted in Figure II-1.

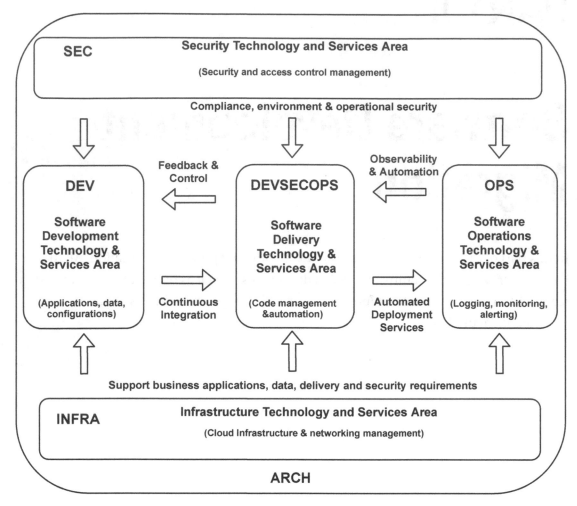

Figure II-1. *Cloud migration technology and services areas*

Chapter 3 begins with a thorough analysis of the application's workloads to ensure you have a thorough understanding of components workload characteristics and their non-functional requirements. The chapter matches those requirements to the cloud provider capabilities and services. Next, you'll see the cloud provider selection process, given business (functional) and architectural (non-functional) requirements, and capture selected cloud migration strategy. To support application migration implementation, we deliver future target architecture artifacts that describe application software components deployment in the cloud provider infrastructure.

After completing the analysis, planning, architecture, and design steps, you'll be ready to build the application infrastructure. In Chapter 4, you'll provision a sound, secure, and cost-efficient cloud environment within Amazon Web Services for application components and database. It will consist of the AWS IAM Service, AWS Elastic Kubernetes Service cluster, and AWS PostgreSQL Relational Database Service (RDS), as well as the underlying virtual networking and storage components.

In Chapter 5, you'll refactor application code, data, and configurations to prepare them for cloud deployment. These changes will be executed manually to build, test, and deploy application components within Docker containers to a Kubernetes cluster, as well as migrate data to the AWS PostgreSQL RDS service. The objective of manual deployment is to develop a hands-on understanding of the changes in regard to relationships between cloud infrastructure, application changes, and deployment process.

In Chapter 6, you'll turn your attention to the concept and implementation of *observability*. You'll see how to select, design, and implement a cloud-native monitoring, logging, alerting solution. All major observability functions will be configured for the entire application technology stack, including infrastructure and application components.

CHAPTER 3

Develop Target Architecture

Out of clutter, find simplicity.
From discord, find harmony.
In the middle of difficulty lies opportunity.

—Albert Einstein

After reading and following the instructions in this chapter, you should be able to accomplish the following objectives:

- Perform application analysis, *document the migration strategy* and *select the cloud provider*.

- Take into consideration and match workload characteristics with cloud provider capabilities to satisfy business (functional) and architectural (non-functional) requirements.

- Deliver *future target architecture* to describe the desired system state for cloud migration.

To address the "when" question, this is the first migration step. It belongs to the planning phase and is performed ahead of actual implementation, see Figure 2-3 in Chapter 2 for reference.

The following roles typically contribute to the activities described in this chapter: Developer, Architect, Network Engineer, Infrastructure Engineer, Operations Engineer, Security Engineer, Quality Analyst, Product Owner, and Agile Master.

© Taras Gleb 2021
T. Gleb, *Systematic Cloud Migration*, https://doi.org/10.1007/978-1-4842-7252-7_3

The migration process starts with extensive research, planning, and analysis. This step is characterized by thorough review and understanding of the current system and its architecture. The review process includes the technology stack, the application component's current state, software versions, the deployment approach, and the runtime environments. Next, the Product and Platform teams have to get familiar with the cloud providers capabilities and services, in order to optimally match application workloads to cloud provider environment and services, and to find the best technology and cost combination of services. This is an important step and must not be skipped, or as the old saying goes "failing to plan is planning to fail". As software developers, we are often guilty of jumping straight into the implementation phase, willingly or under delivery pressure. To help with planning and analysis, this book provides a list of recommended inputs and outputs. Keep in mind that the document content should be adapted to suit a particular migration scenario or specific functional and non-functional requirements.

To get you started, the following cloud-native methodologies and frameworks provide a solid foundation to design the future state architecture.

- *Evolutionary architecture:* Supports guided, incremental, and controlled (via fitness functions) change along important system dimensions (Source: ThoughtWorks).

- *Cloud-native architecture:* Designed for automation, is stateless, favors managed services, cloud-native, and open-source technologies, practices defense-in-depth security and evolutionary architecture (Source: Google).

- *Cloud architecture principles:* Follows industry and vendor best practices and architecture principles, such as AWS Well-Architectured Pillars and Azure Well Architected Framework.

Inputs

To deliver effective, cost-efficient, and secure cloud solutions, we start by analyzing a current state architecture, as well as the functional and non-functional requirements. It is important to review how current business processes and functions are supported by the existing system, including who the system users are, what interfaces exist between the systems and system's components, what data flows exist, and what data stores are being used to persist configuration, operational, and historical data. Typical inputs include:

- *Application cloud migration objectives*: Although there is some commonality across many applications, each product objectives may have context specific set. For the demo application in this book, the objectives are straightforward: build a cost-efficient and secure cloud environment, refactor the code to migrate the application utilizing the CICD automated approach, and take advantage of cloud computing characteristics such as elasticity, automation, and innovation to enable efficient and high-quality cloud operations.

- *Application business (functional) requirements*: In this case, support current business processes and functions.

- *Application architectural (non-functional) requirements*: There is a standard set of architectural requirements adapted to the cloud, that we seek to meet in this migration: reliability, availability, maintainability, reliability, performance, security, extendibility, manageability, and cost-efficiency.

- *Other*: Any organization, compliance, government or migration-specific standards, or guidelines, as well as business or technology related documentation.

Process and Activities

To analyze and produce output, the software architect and team needs to organize requirements elicitation meetings, brainstorming and joint design sessions, also known as *architecture katas, a*s part of the planning activities. The objective is to ensure that the requirements, constraints, and risk are collected from the broad pool of the organizational stakeholders, and there are no gaps in business, technology, security, compliance, and operational requirements.

A *cloud architect,* who is the leading resource in this step, must have a clear understanding of the system's current state and business processes it supports. If possible, request a demo of the system to understand the system flow. Reach out and communicate with other Product and Platform teams, production support, operations, customer service representatives, and account managers in order to create all-inclusive architecture views of the current state of the system under migration.

This approach helps uncover any current or future dependencies, integration points, and regulatory and other requirements that might greatly impact architecture decisions, choices, and outcomes.

Output and Deliverables

The deliverables section starts with a standard architecture artifact: *Solution Architecture Document (SAD)*. This artifact is a living document and canonical source of truth about your software application. For the sake of brevity, we will limit SAD content in this chapter only to relevant diagrams (views), such as combined *components, and deployment views*. The list of deliverables could include the following documents:

- Solution Architecture Document (SAD)
- Cloud Provider Selection Matrix
- Proposed Target State Architecture (as part of SAD)
- Components Change Summary
- Risk Analysis Document
- Resource Capacity and Cost Planning

In the following sections, we will work together on each deliverable to demonstrate how to approach and create these outputs, and how to ensure they are relevant and beneficial to the migration process. This is the preliminary phase of the analysis and there are a lot of *unknown unknowns*, which could be challenging, demand extensive research, and create mental and process blocks.

The important part is to continue iterations with analysis and use the 80/20 rule, before moving on or making a decision, as it is virtually impossible to have all the information upfront. The evolutionary architecture methodology applied in this text is well suited and very helpful for this approach.

Review Current State Architecture

The current state architecture for our sample application is depicted in Figure 3-1 (as combined component and deployment diagram), where the source code for it is available on GitHub repository via the book's product page, located at *www.apress.com/ 9781484272510*. The application provides hands-on code examples and adds practical aspects to understanding the cloud migration concepts and implementation details. It consists of four tiers: Client (any desktop or mobile browser), Web (JavaScript, HTML, CSS and Angular Framework), Business (Java Spring Boot Framework), and Data (PostgreSQL RDBMS Database). Values in parentheses describe implementation technologies.

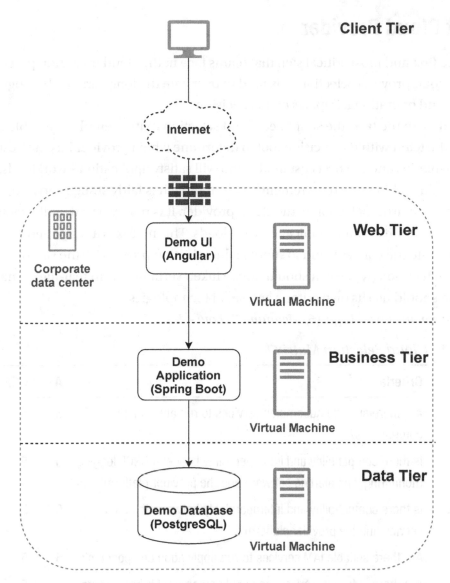

Figure 3-1. *Current state components and deployment architecture*

It is a typical n-tier web application, where each tier is responsible for a subset of functions and implemented with commonly used technologies. This view offers sufficient information to start the public cloud provider selection process. There are no specific requirements or constraints within the application, which in turn gives us a wide range of choices in regard to cloud providers, services and underlying technologies.

Select Cloud Provider

One of the first and most critical step that teams face in the cloud migration process, is public cloud provider selection. It is hard to overstate the long-term technology, financial, and operational impacts of this decision.

To help with the task, the simplified cloud selection matrix template in Table 3-1 provides the team with the decision tool to determine which provider has the best set of capabilities and the best cost model and will satisfy application's workloads, business, and architecture requirements. This approach is fairly straightforward, as it allows for impartial selection of the cloud provider. It is purely based on the cloud provider's suitability for the application workloads. This matrix is a simplified example to demonstrate the concept, and to support the selection process for the sample application technology stack. It should not be taken verbatim, as in real-life scenario each team should use its own criteria and set of technologies.

Requirements met = High - 5, Medium - 2, Low – 1

Table 3-1. *Cloud Selection Matrix*

Area	Criteria	AWS	GCP	Azure
Dev	Are there suitable Kubernetes services to run application components?	5	5	5
Ops	Is there compatibility and interoperability between CNCF logging, monitoring, and alerting software and the provider platform?	5	5	2
DevSecOps	Is there compatibility and interoperability between the GitLab service and the provider platform?	5	2	1
Sec	Are there suitable IAM services to run application components?	5	5	5
Infra	Are there sufficient services to enable automated infrastructure deployments?	5	5	5
Total		25	22	18

As you can see, this totally fictitious selection process pointed to AWS as the cloud provider of choice. A quick disclaimer: these numbers are purely for demonstration purposes only, to assist in explaining the process. They do not reflect any actual provider's capabilities. With cloud provider selection completed, we are ready to move on to the migration strategy selection from the list of available choices.

Select Migration Strategy

Another important set of choices is migration strategy selection. Various migration strategies, as well as guiding principles on how to apply these strategies, were introduced in Chapter 2, Table 2-2.

To take full advantage of the latest cloud-native technologies for our sample application, and to benefit from cloud provider services, we choose Replatform strategy for application components, both user interface and backend and select Repurchase strategy for the database, as depicted in Table 3-2.

Table 3-2. *Migration Strategy Selection*

Component	Migration Strategy	Delivery Model	Maturity Model
Demo UI Web Application (Angular)	**Replatform (Lift & Reshape)** Change underlying platform, runtime, middleware, framework, package into container.	PaaS	Cloud-ready Cloud-friendly Cloud-native
Demo Business Application (Spring Boot)	**Replatform (Lift & Reshape)** Change underlying platform, runtime, middleware, framework, package into container.	PaaS	Cloud-ready Cloud-friendly Cloud-native
Demo Database (PostgreSQL)	**Repurchase** Replace with commercial-off-the-shelf (COTS) or SaaS.	SaaS	Cloud-ready Cloud-friendly Cloud-native

These strategies seem to be well-suited for our sample application, and allow the teams take full advantage of cloud provider managed services, delegating non-value adding activities to the platform, while keeping the cost down on the Kubernetes cluster. Additionally, deploying application components to the Kubernetes cluster provides automation and elasticity to scale applications up and down, to match the workloads, which could be quite unpredictable with the web application component.

After cloud providers and future migration technologies are selected, we have sufficient inputs to start designing the future proposed target state architecture.

Propose Target State Architecture

The team has found AWS to be the most suitable cloud provider, and a Docker container running on a Kubernetes cluster to be an adequate technology stack for Web Tier and Business Tier components. This approach will provide the following benefits: agility (deploy faster), portability (move workloads with ease between different environments or providers), density (cost and resource utilization efficiency), elasticity and scalability (match workloads and resources and provide automated up and down resource provisioning). The solution is cloud-native, vendor-agnostic, cost-efficient, and supported by the open-source community.

AWS PostgreSQL managed service was selected as the future technology for the application data. It has demonstrated good performance, security and reliability characteristics, and the team should benefit from provider-managed data management services, such as back-up, replication and failover.

Cross-cutting concerns, such as logging and monitoring, are implemented using Elasticsearch, FluentBit and Kibana or EfK stack. Applications will utilize Prometheus and Grafana for metrics collection and visualization. The alerting functionality will be provided by PagerDuty Software as a Service.

This architecture fully adheres to Chapter 2 cloud-native design principles to ensure we deliver future-proof, sound, and evolutionary solutions. All the choices are illustrated in the future target state architecture in Figure 3-2.

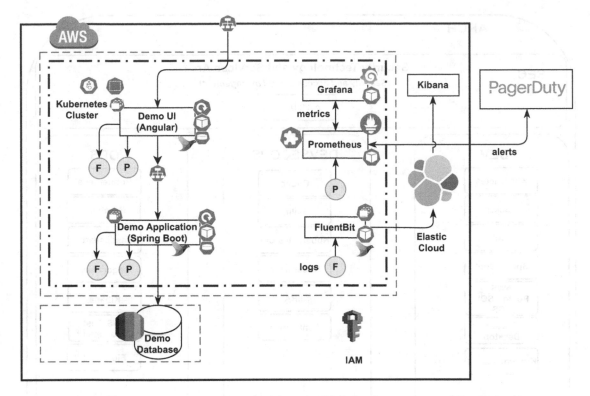

Figure 3-2. *Future target state components and deployment architecture*

We have made very good progress so far and have answered the majority of the questions as to who the cloud provider of choice is, what migration strategies are selected, and how our future state architecture looks. We have both baseline and future state architecture at our disposal, and we are ready to build a roadmap and analyze what changes are required for each tier and tier components to arrive at the desired future state.

Analyze Components Change Summary

In this section, we determine a components change summary for each of the five technology and service areas of the sample application. It is a four-tiered web based application running HTML, CSS, and Angular in the client tier, Java Spring Boot in the business tier, and PostgreSQL in the data tier. Every team's technology stack will be different, and so the technologies selected. However, using these areas, guiding principles, and selection criteria should be sufficient to assist teams in choosing the best tool for the job for every scenario and stack. See Figure 3-3.

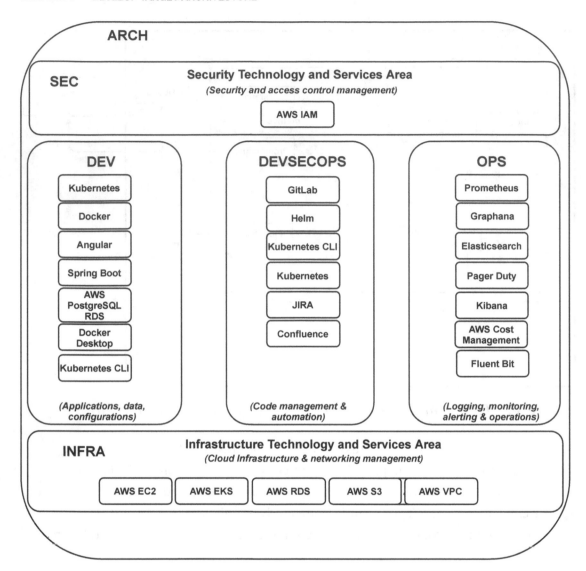

Figure 3-3. *Sample application cloud technologies*

Table 3-3 lists all the application components, matches them to the selected technologies, and includes a brief description summary of change for the migration. It also conveniently groups these components by technology and service knowledge areas.

Table 3-3. *Component Change Summary*

Area	Component	Technology	Summary of Change
Dev	Demo Application UI	Angular, HTML, CSS, JavaScript	Package application into Docker container.
Dev	Demo Application Back-end Service	Java Spring Boot	Package application into Docker container.
Dev	Demo Application Database	AWS PostgreSQL RDS	Deploy the database as a cloud provider managed service.
Ops	Prometheus Metrics Stack	Prometheus, Grafana	Deploy the Prometheus Operator into a Kubernetes cluster.
Ops	Elasticsearch Logging Stack	Elasticsearch, Kibana, Fluent Bit	Provision a cloud elastic service on the cloud provider infrastructure.
Ops	Pager Duty	Pager Duty SaaS	Create a Pager Duty configuration for the application.
DevSecOps	GitLab, JIRA, Confluence	Integrated CICD Platform and workflow and knowledge tools	Create code repositories and develop a CICD pipeline.
Infra	AWS VPC, AWS EKS, AWS S3, AWS EC2	AWS EKS	Create an AWS infrastructure including VPC, EC2 and EKS Kubernetes Cluster to deploy application components.
Sec	AWS IAM	AWS IAM	Create RBAC roles to build an AWS infrastructure and deploy application components and data into the environment.

We have sufficient information now to start analyzing risks that might arise, given the required changes to be completed for migration.

Complete Risk Log

The *Risk Log* identifies risks for each technology and service migration area and proposes the mitigation strategies. The sample Risk Log document shown in Table 3-4 is focused on risk impact, probability, and available mitigation strategies. For brevity, there are a very few sample entries in the template. Real-life scenarios call for many more identifiable risks that are application, team, business, and context specific, and these files are hundreds of items long. It is beneficial to circulate this document across a wide variety of stakeholders within the organization and capture related risks.

Each entry in Table 3-4 is classified using a numerical value to characterize probability and impact. This approach will help teams organize and order risks and mitigation strategies.

Impact = High - 5, Medium - 2, Low – 1
Probability = High - 5, Medium - 2, Low – 1

Table 3-4. *Risk Log*

Risk Area	Impact Description	Impact	Probability	Mitigation Strategy
Dev	An evolving technology that might require the team to upgrade or rearchitect a solution.	2	2	Select future-proof technologies and architecture to minimize the need to upgrade or rearchitect.
Ops	Service reliability and uptime.	5	1	Design vendor-agnostic DR solution with automated failure detection and failover.
DevSecOps	Pipeline software will not work with the cloud provider infrastructure.	1	1	Migrate to cloud provider's CICD technology or deploy manually.
Sec	Verify the use of a secure software development lifecycle that addresses security in all stages of development.	5	5	Implement secure software testing procedures in the CICD pipeline.

Risks and related mitigation strategies are conveniently grouped by technology and service knowledge areas. We are now ready to move on to resource planning and cost analysis, which should be a mandatory step in any cloud migration.

Conduct Cost Analysis

Cloud migration planning would be deficient without upfront cost planning activities. Resource requirements and cost analysis should be solution design criteria, not an optimization afterthought. In general, a lot of teams take the opposite approach, which leads to cost overruns and results in an expensive solution that takes a very long time to optimize or eventually forces them to refactor the solution altogether. Also, this approach fits into cloud-native architecture principle of building cost-conscious organizations.

Cloud providers offer cost calculators to estimate the total cost of the designed solution on a monthly or annual basis, including breakdown per tier, component, or service. There are a variety of methodologies and third-party software solutions, in terms of how to calculate the solution costs in the cloud. An example of rudimentary rule-of-thumb calculation methodology is to imagine deploying application components onto the cloud provider's virtual machines in a one-to-one fashion, one datacenter virtual machine for one provider virtual machine, matching CPU, RAM, and HD parameters. Then, price provider's machines and derive the total cloud cost. You can also cloud compare solution costs to corporate datacenter costs, on as-is or lift-and-shift basis.

One advantage of such a calculation is the "apple-to-apple" comparison, even though there could be minor deviations in hardware characteristics between corporate and cloud provider's virtual machines. This is the first approximation for our cost analysis and will be refined during the implementation, when we receive actual reporting information after the deployment. See Table 3-5.

Table 3-5. *Cost Analysis Sample*

Component	Cloud Resource	Cost per Unit (USD/Month)	Total (USD/Month)
Demo Web Application	AWS EKS Cluster	$50	$50
Demo Business Application	AWS EKS Cluster	$50	$50
Demo Database	AWS RDS Service	$75	$75
Total			$175

Note   Each cloud provider has free-tier services; refer to the provider's documentation pages for more information.

Tools, Techniques and Best Practices

This section provides reference materials to support architecture, design, implementation, and operation of cloud-native, cost-efficient solutions (in the Arch technology and services area). The idea behind the list is that these technologies, tools, or techniques are aligned with the cloud migration design principles and allow the team to take full advantage of the cloud deployment model, the cloud services model, the migration strategies, and the cloud computing characteristics. See Table 3-6.

Often teams consult the cloud-provider's architecture, technical, and on-boarding teams during migration. It definitely helps to understand the available services and best practices, as there is a wealth of information and provider teams can help navigate that informational space. However, the solutions presented by the vendor technologists should be viewed as one of available alternative and evaluated in the context of the team's migration objectives and architecture principles—e.g., are they cloud-agnostic or cost-efficient. Don't take them verbatim because the cloud provider architecture teams are often limited in their knowledge of the application requirements and what are the alternative open source or competitor technologies.

Table 3-6. *Tools, Techniques, and Best Practices*

Tool/Technique/Best Practice	Description and Benefits
AWS Well Architected Framework	Set of guidelines to implement high-quality solutions on the AWS platform.
Azure Well Architected Framework	Set of guidelines to implement high-quality solutions on the Azure platform.
Cloudockit	Architecture visualization and automation tool to generate fully editable diagrams of the cloud or on-premise environment.
Cloud-Native Architecture	Designed for automation, favors managed services, cloud-native, and open-source technologies, practices defense-in-depth security and evolutionary architecture.
Cloud-Native Application Bundle	A spec for building, installing, and managing container native applications.

(continued)

Table 3-6. (*continued*)

Tool/Technique/Best Practice	Description and Benefits
Cloud-Native Application Development	An approach to application design, development, and operations that allows teams to take full advantage of the cloud computing model.
Cloud-Native Computing Foundation	Vendor-neutral incubator for cloud-native open-source projects.
Cloud Journey Tracker (Azure)	Discover and document the cloud adoption journey based on strategic business requirements.
Cloud run cost Architecture Fitness Function	Fitness functions are introduced as part of the evolutionary architecture. It's extremely important to implement this early on.
Cloud Pilot	Static code analysis tool to determine application code cloud-readiness.
Everything as a Service	Cloud solution design principle to implement application, data, infrastructure, and DR as a service.
Evolutionary Architecture	Architecture approach that promotes system design and enables incremental controlled change via fitness functions.
Google Drawio	Visualization tool to create diagrams, workflows, and other materials to help understand information and processes to drive better decisions.
Google Well Architected Framework	Set of guidelines to implement high-quality solutions on the Google platform.
Lucidcharts	Visualization tool to create diagrams, workflows, and other materials to help understand information and process to drive better decisions.
RedHat Migration Toolkit	Java applications cloud migration code analysis tool.
Services Based Architecture	Provides significant advantages over a monolithic architecture that includes better scalability, decoupling, and control over development, testing, and deployment.

This table is a good starting point into cloud technologies, methodologies, and industry accepted best practices. It provides you with comprehensive and systematic information that can support and drive any major decision your team may face during cloud migration.

Summary

This chapter explained *the migration planning and preparation activities*, and you're now ready to start the *migration implementation*. You performed application *workload analysis*, selected and *documented the migration strategy*, including the *cloud provider*, based on best fit between application workloads and cloud provider capabilities.

The chapter also documented the *future state architecture*. It also analyzed changes to the application, data, and configuration to prepare the code for the cloud. It discussed how to conduct high-level relative *cost analysis* to ensure cost efficiency.

You should now be ready to move onto building a cloud environment for the sample application.

CHAPTER 4

Build Secure Cloud Environment

I don't need a hard disk in my computer if I can get to the server faster... carrying around these non-connected computers is byzantine by comparison.

— Steve Jobs

After reading and following the instructions in this chapter, you should be able to accomplish the following objectives:

- Build a *robust, secure, and cost-efficient cloud environment* in AWS for the application components and the database, consisting of IAM services, an AWS EKS cluster, PostgreSQL RDS SaaS, AWS VPC, networking, and AWS S3 storage.

- Secure the cluster, the database service, the network, and the storage.

To address the "when" question; this is the first step in migration implementation. It belongs to the implementation phase, after planning and design steps have been completed. See Chapter 2, Figure 2-3, for reference.

The following roles typically contribute to the activities described in this chapter: Developer, Architect, Network Engineer, Infrastructure Engineer, Operations Engineer, Security Engineer, Quality Analyst, Product Owner, and Agile Master.

With the planning and design activities completed, we can now start the implementation. This chapter covers provisioning and configuring the AWS cloud infrastructure to support future deployment of application components and data. The environment consists of identity and access control, networking infrastructure, Kubernetes cluster, PostgreSQL RDS SaaS, and mandatory security configurations.

57

© Taras Gleb 2021
T. Gleb, *Systematic Cloud Migration*, https://doi.org/10.1007/978-1-4842-7252-7_4

For user interface and business tier components, we provision AWS Elastic Kubernetes Service (EKS). It offers value-added benefits in deployment, management, security and automation for infrastructure, application components as well as seamless integration with other AWS services. EKS reduces cluster administration effort and automates availability and scalability of Kubernetes control plane, which is non-business-value activity, while being administration heavy and knowledge intensive proposition.

Given that we deploy UI and business components inside a Docker container, EKS offers automated scalability to match variable workloads for the cluster infrastructure and application components running within it. It takes care of container and orchestration workflows for any containerized components: application, data, storage, logging, and networking. EKS infrastructure capabilities are aligned and supportive of the chosen technology stack, future target state architecture, cloud characteristics and migration requirements in regard to cost, timelines, and the team's skillset. AWS EKS supports and simplifies the cloud-native architecture and applications.

For the data tier, the Product team provisions AWS PostgreSQL RDS in a self-service manner that is coherent with the cloud computing concept and the cloud shared responsibility model. This approach is agile from the Product team's perspective, as the team is decoupled and has no dependency on the Platform team to create the service. We take advantage of the pricing elasticity feature, and for the purposes of this book, we are provisioning the free-tier RDS service. You can configure any desired PostgreSQL version, including the latest available on AWS. The service provides data backup, replication, and any additional data and software management utilities out of the box. The service permits team focus on implementing value-added business code and delegating low-value administrative tasks to the cloud provider service.

Our cloud environment infrastructure, services, application, and data will be properly secured during implementation, as cloud security is not an afterthought. In terms of security implementation, teams benefit from the shared responsibility model, where the provider is responsible for the *security of the cloud*, including its physical infrastructure and the compute, storage, and networking components. The team is responsible for the *security in the cloud*, including configuration of the cluster data plane (security groups control traffic from the AWS EKS control plane into the VPC), nodes, containers, firewall rules, and identity and access management.

Application data will be protected by data encryption in-flight via SSL/TLS and at-rest via disk-level encryption. AWS security services provide Security as a Service (SECaaS) for automation, consistency, and high-reliability. In addition, we follow Zero

Trust security mode, where the network security access model is based on strict identity verification processes. Finally, the Defense in Depth principle relies on multiple lines of defense, hardened security, and layers of isolation across clusters, networks, and data services.

Inputs

To build a robust and secure cloud environment, you need application technical documentation with up-to-date infrastructure configurations, resource requirements, and deployment descriptions. Some documents are provided as output of the previous planning step, e.g. future target state architecture. The following list is simply an example of what we are going to use. Documents and content could vary for each team's migration scenario or business and architecture requirements:

- Current state architecture

- Future target state architecture

- Components change summary

- Risk analysis document

- Cloud resources naming and tagging

- Resource capacity and cost planning

- Existing infrastructure configurations and resource requirements, such as CPU (cores), RAM (GB), and HD (GB, type HDD, SSD)

- Network traffic volume

- Runtime performance analysis

- RBAC matrix:

  - Security roles and groups

  - Access matrix for authentication/authorization and resource access linked to the enterprise user management or identity system

Process and Activities

This section covers building and securing the cloud infrastructure and provisioning the required services—Amazon EKS Kubernetes Cluster and Amazon PostgreSQL RDS. There are tools that users must install on the local machine first. In the context of the shared responsibility model between the Product and Platform teams, the following separation of duties is recommended. Tasks related to AWS account creation, infrastructure, and network setup, IAM administrator roles creation cluster creation are performed by the Platform team. The Product team will be concerned with local machine configuration and database related service activities. This separation of duties is just a proposed example and may vary in real life, depending on the skillset of each team.

Note   To follow the environment parity principle of the Twelve Factor App methodology, the Dev, QA, UAT, Prod, and DR environments should be as identical as possible. That way, teams can reuse deployment artifacts, support automation, and eliminate error-prone manual deployment and configuration steps.

Prerequisites

The following software needs to be installed locally or configured within cloud provider services before continuing to build the cloud environment infrastructure:

- AWS Account to work with AWS resources

- AWS CLI command-line tool to work with AWS resources

- Kubernetes resources (see *https://kubernetes.io/docs/ tutorials/kubernetes-basics/*)

- kubectl command-line tool to work with local and AWS clusters

- minikube local Kubernetes development tool to run a single-node cluster inside a virtual machine

You need an active AWS account to perform the activities in this chapter. If you have one, you can skip this step. Otherwise, navigate to the sign-up page at *https://portal. aws.amazon.com/billing/signup* and follow the instructions. Note the Access Key ID and Secret Access Key, as you will need them during configuration.

Additional software is required on your machine to access Amazon resources after you have created and AWS account. Use the links below and complete the installation tasks for the AWS Command Line Interface (CLI) and kubectl utilities.

After AWS CLI has been installed, you can configure login credentials. The fastest way to accomplish this is to open a local terminal window, execute **aws configure** command in the terminal, and follow the prompts (additional information is available on the "Configuring the AWS CLI" documentation page at *https://docs.aws .amazon.com/cli/latest/userguide/cli-chap-configure.html*).

AWS will ask for the Access Key ID, the Secret Access Key, the AWS Region, and the Output Format. The first two variables were created during the account selection process and last two are selected during configuration. This information is stored in the default profile within the credentials file.

AWS Elastic Kubernetes Service (EKS) Cluster

The cluster creation process has been split into two steps. First, we provision the cluster prerequisites: AWS Virtual Private Cloud (VPC) and Cluster IAM Role. Then, we create and configure the AWS EKS cluster itself. Additionally, there are two approaches to create a new cluster in Amazon EKS; use the **eksctl** command (the command-line utility provided by Amazon, which is probably the fastest way), or use the AWS Management Console and AWS CLI. To present deeper insight into the resource creation process and to illustrate how resources work together, we will use the console option.

Note   In a large enterprise, the environment cluster could be provisioned by platform teams (Security, System, and Network Engineers), using an IaC approach, with the code stored in a repository.

Create Virtual Private Cloud (VPC)

Before we launch AWS EKS, we need to provision the Virtual Private Cloud (VPC) service. This virtual network is similar to traditional datacenter networks. It represents a logically isolated section of the AWS datacenter network, with the added benefit of cloud provider infrastructure scalability.

It is recommended to create a VPC with both public and private subnets to enable Internet access and load balancing in public subnets, while placing security-sensitive backend components and data into private subnets. All subnets will be deployed to the same AWS availability zone. This service could be created via the Amazon command line interface or using the AWS web console. Another alternative is the AWS cloud formation template, which provides out-of-the-box control plane and node security group configurations with AWS recommended settings. We will use this method, as it is the fastest and allows us to benefit from best practices and opinionated AWS configurations.

To provision VPC, navigate to AWS CloudFormation console at *https://console .aws.amazon.com/cloudformation* and follow these steps:

1. Ensure that you pick a *Region* in the navigation bar that supports Amazon EKS. Select **Create Stack, With New Resources (Standard)**. For the template, click **Choose a Template**, select **Specify an Amazon S3 Template URL**, and insert the following URL below into the text area. Click **Next** when you're done:

   https://s3.us-west-2.amazonaws.com/amazon-eks/ cloudformation/2020-10-29/amazon-eks-vpc-private- subnets.yaml

2. Complete the parameters on the **Specify Details** page and then click **Next**. Keep in mind that the default values provide a sufficient amount of IP addresses for the implementation; however, you can configure your own values.

   • *Stack name*: Select a stack name for AWS CloudFormation

   • *VpcBlock*: Pick a CIDR range for Kubernetes nodes, pods, and load balancers that are assigned an IP addresses from this block.

- *PublicSubnet01Block* **and** *PublicSubnet02Block*: Choose a CIDR block for public subnet 1 and 2.

- *PrivateSubnet01Block* **and** *PrivateSubnet02Block*: Specify a CIDR block for private subnet 1 and 2.

3. From the *Options* page, tag your stack resources (optional), and then choose **Next**. From the *Review* page, select **Create**.

4. After the stack is provisioned, select the console and pick **Outputs**. Record the following values for EKS cluster creation. They can also be located on the *VPC Service in AWS Console*.

- *SecurityGroups*: The security group ID applied to the elastic network interfaces.

- *VpcId*: For launching the node group template.

- *SubnetIds*: Subnet IDs to launch the nodes into.

Now we have a VPC with two public and two private subnets ready for the AWS EKS cluster. If you need additional information, see the AWS documentation page at *https://docs.aws.amazon.com/eks/latest/userguide/create-public-private-vpc .html*.

Create Identity Access Management (IAM) Role

To allow the EKS cluster to securely invoke other AWS services, we need a suitable cluster IAM role. When the role is created, it has to be assigned a set of permissions or IAM policies: the AmazonEKSClusterPolicy. We can use an AWS Identity and Access Management (IAM) service that controls access to AWS resources for authentication and authorization (this service is free of charge) and provides role and policy management capabilities.

We can use the following steps to first verify if the account has the role and whether the role has AmazonEKSClusterPolicy attached. If the answer is yes, we can skip to the next section,; otherwise, we need to create the role and attach the correct policies. Navigate to the IAM Console at *https://console.aws.amazon.com/iam/*, then follow these steps:

1. Choose *Roles* in the navigation panel and look for *eksClusterRole* in the list. If the role does not exist, move on to Step 3.

2. If the role has been successfully located, select and verify the role's policies, which is *AmazonEKSClusterPolicy.* If the policy has been attached, the role is correctly configured and you can skip the rest of the steps.

3. To create a new role, choose **Create Role**, then **EKS** in the list of services and *EKS Cluster* for our scenario.

   a. Select *Permissions*, then **Next**: *Tags*. You can add key-value metadata tags; however, this step is optional.

   b. Click **Next**: Review, type a unique name for the role, and then select **Create Role**.

If you need additional information on how to create or configure the role, visit the AWS documentation page at https://docs.aws.amazon.com/eks/latest/userguide/ service_IAM_role.html.

Create AWS EKS Cluster

After you have successfully completed the cluster prerequisites, the next step is to create the cluster using the AWS Management Console. At the end of this process, you will have a Kubernetes cluster ready for deployment of our sample application components.

1. Navigate to *https://console.aws.amazon.com/eks/home#/ clusters* and click the **Create Cluster** button. Fill in the required fields on the *Configure Cluster* page:

   a. *Name*: Name of the cluster

   b. Kubernetes version

     c. *Cluster service role*: Select the IAM role created in the prerequisite step. For more information, see *https://docs.aws.amazon.com/eks/latest/userguide/add-user-role.html*.

2. Click the **Next** button. On the *Specify Networking* page, select values from the following fields:

     a. *VPC*: The VPC created in the prerequisite step

     b. *Subnets*: Available subnets from the previously created VPC; by default, there are four subnets available in the default VPC for the cluster nodes to be placed into

     c. *Security Groups*: Values from AWS Cloud Formation Output generated during the VPC creation step

     d. *Cluster Endpoint Access*: There are three options:

         i. *Public*: Enables public access to the Kubernetes API Cluster

        ii. *Private*: Enables only private access to the Kubernetes API Cluster

      iii. *Public and Private*: Enables both types of access

3. Click the **Next** button. You can choose the type of logging from the *Configure Logging* page or leave it as Disabled to later add your own logging mechanism.

4. Click the **Next** button. On the *Review and Create* page, review the information you entered. You need to update the *kubeconfig* file to connect to the newly created cluster. The most convenient way to do this is to use the AWS CLI **update-kubeconfig** command; see update-kubeconfig in the AWS CLI Command Reference.

We have created an AWS EKS cluster and at this point we have its control plane up and running, as shown in Figure 4-1.

Figure 4-1. *The AWS EKS cluster*

However, we are still missing data plane compute resources for the worker nodes inside the newly created EKS cluster, which is where we will deploy the application containers. There are two options:

- *Fargate (Linux OS)*: Suitable for running Linux applications deployed to AWS Fargate.

- *Managed Nodes (Linux OS)*: Suitable for running either Linux or Windows applications on an Amazon EC2 instance.

To stay away from the copy-paste approach, we provide a link to the AWS documentation URL to follow the steps. Navigate to the *Getting Started with Amazon EKS* – AWS Management Console and *AWS CLI* page (`https://docs.aws.amazon.com/eks/latest/userguide/getting-started-console.html`). Scroll to Step 4: Create Nodes I Managed Nodes Linux tab and follow the directions to create compute nodes for the Kubernetes cluster.

Now that you have successfully provisioned a Kubernetes cluster, added worker Nodes and started it, the next step is to connect to it from your machine's Kubernetes client. Execute the command in Listing 4-1 to update a local *kubeconfig* file with your cluster context. You should receive confirmation on the command line.

Listing 4-1. Updating the Local kubeconfig File

```
$ aws eks update-kubeconfig --region us-east-2 --name demo-aws-eks-cluster
Added new context arn:aws:eks:us-east-2:785530736506:cluster/demo-aws-eks-
cluster to C:\Users\<user>\.kube\config
```

You can verify that the configuration file was updated successfully by executing the command in Listing 4-2. The output confirms that your local context has been set with your AWS cluster.

Listing 4-2. Verifying That the Configuration File Was Updated Successfully

```
$kubectl config current-context
arn:aws:eks:us-east-2:785530736506:cluster/demo-aws-eks-cluster
```

Alternatively, connect to the cluster and verify services by executing the command in Listing 4-3. Output confirms that the connection is successful and you can connect to the Kubernetes server API.

Listing 4-3. Verifying the Cluster Services

```
$kubectl get svc
NAME     TYPE CLUSTER-IP     EXTERNAL-IP PORT(S) AGE
kubernetes ClusterIP 10.100.0.1 <none> 443/TCP 5d8h
```

We deploy application components in subsequent chapters. However, it is good housekeeping practice to delete any resources no longer required to save cost. If you need to, in order to delete the cluster, navigate to the *Amazon EKS* console at *https:// console.aws.amazon.com/eks/home#/clusters*, choose the cluster, and click **Delete**. Enter a cluster name on the confirmation screen and click **Delete**.

At this point, your cluster is up and running and ready to accept connections and application deployments.

Security

Running a Kubernetes cluster in AWS provides benefits from the cloud shared security responsibility model. AWS is responsible for control plane security, which contains master nodes and etcd storage components. It is tested regularly during the AWS Compliance Program verification runs.

The Product team is responsible for data plane security configuration of the security groups that control traffic from the AWS EKS control plane to the customer's VPC. In a production environment, extra configurations are required for the nodes and containers, as well as network security, with firewall rules to manage network traffic. Fine-grained access control, identity management, authentication, and authorization are provided by the IAM role. We only scratched the surface in regard to security configurations, as they are outside of the scope of this book. However, additional resources are provided in the "Tools, Techniques and Best Practices" section.

Next, we are ready to move to provisioning the AWS PostgreSQL Relational Database Service.

Create PostgreSQL Database Service

The team selected self-service SaaS for the data tier. It is represented by the AWS PostgreSQL Relational Database Service, which will be provisioned as a deliverable for this section. Additional choices in regard to cloud maturity and delivery models are:

- *Run database inside Docker container*: When the cloud provider database service is not available or cannot be used for technical or business reasons, then a containerized database is a viable option. Containerized databases could be used during testing as part of the DevSecOps pipeline.

- *Run self-managed database on cloud provider VM*: This is a low cloud maturity approach and is not being considered in this book. It could be a viable option for particular requirements, e.g., if you require access to the root user.

The fundamental building block of Amazon RDS is the database instance. The database instance can be accessed via a network address or endpoint, which our sample application will use to connect to. Before you create the instance, some consideration should be given to the following requirements:

- *Database engine type*: Choose PostgreSQL for this example.

- *Networking*: Select default, user-defined, or no VPC.

- *High availability*: Configure failover support and whether backup DB is configured within a single or multiple Availability Zone(s).

- *Memory, storage size, and type*: Choose Magnetic (Standard Storage), General Purpose (SSD), or Provisioned IOPS (PIOPS) storage type.

- *Security practices*: Separate IAM roles, SSL data access, and disk encryption for in-transit and at-rest data protection.Keep in mind that real-life projects may have additional requirements. The Amazon PostgreSQL RDS created in this section will be "free tier". On one hand, free tier is missing some critical production-grade capabilities and is typically smaller in size; on the other hand, the "free tier" option is a good starting point to get familiar with the platform without breaking the bank.Our PostgreSQL instance will be `db.t2.micro` DB instance; 20GB of storage, automated backups enabled, with a retention period of one day (all of this is "free-tier" eligible).To create the service, open the AWS Management Console (`https://console.aws.amazon.com/console/`) and follow these steps:

1. Select *RDS* and the *region* in which the service will be created. Make sure you select the same region as the AWS EKS cluster to avoid incurring networking charges and latency issues. In the *Create Database Section*, choose **Create Database**. Select the database engine (in our case, it's PostgreSQL) and choose Only Enable Options Eligible for RDS Free Usage Tier.

2. Click the **Next** button, and in the *Configuration Settings*, enter the following:

   a. *License model*: Default, postgresql-license

   b. *DB engine version*: Default

   c. *DB instance class*: The default, db.t2.micro

   d. *Multi-AZ deployment*: Multi-AZ Deployment is not part of free tier. This mode automatically provisions and maintains a synchronous standby replica in a different Availability Zone

   e. *Storage type*: General Purpose (SSD)

   f. *Allocated storage*: Default of 20 to allocate 20GB of storage

g. *Enable storage autoscaling*: You can use this feature to enable RDS to automatically scale up your storage when needed. Not part of free tier

h. *DB instance identifier*: Name for the DB instance

i. *Master username*: A username to log in to your DB instance

j. *Master password*: A password that contains from 8 to 41 characters

k. *Confirm password*: Reenter your password

3. Click the **Next** button. In the *Advanced Settings*, enter the following for each section.

Network and Security Section:

a. *Virtual private cloud*: Default VPC

b. *Subnet group*: The default subnet group

c. *Public accessibility*: No

d. *Availability zone*: No preference

e. *VPC security groups*: Create new VPC security group to allow connection

f. *Encryption*: Not available in the free tier

Database Options Section:

a. *Database name*: A database name

b. *Port*: The default value of 5432

c. *DB parameter group*: Default value

d. *Option group: Not available in the free tier*

e. *IAM DB authentication*: Choose Disable. This option allows you to manage your database credentials through AWS IAM users and groups

Backup Section:

> a. *Backup retention period*: The number of days to retain the backup; set this value to 1 day
>
> b. *Backup window*: Default of no preferences

Monitoring Section:

> a. *Enhanced monitoring*: Choose Enable Enhanced Monitoring to see metrics in real time

Maintenance Section:

> a. *Auto minor version upgrade*: Choose Enable Auto Minor Version Upgrade to update automatically
>
> b. *Maintenance window*: Choose No Preference

Deletion Protection Section:

> a. *Enable deletion protection*: When enabled, database can't be deleted

- The list of service configuration options is extensive, and there are more choices which are outside of free tier and could also be configured via CLI as opposed to a web interface. It may take a few minutes to complete the service creation. Once it's ready, you will be presented with the screen shown in Figure 4-2.

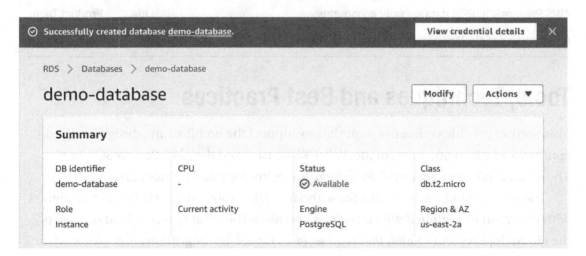

Figure 4-2. *The AWS PostgreSQL RDS*

At this time, you have the database service configured and available via the HTTPS service endpoint, which adheres to the 12-factor application methodology. You can familiarize yourself with the various editable configuration options available in the service.

Output and Deliverables

Table 4-1 provides a list of deliverables required to migrate application components and data to the cloud provider infrastructure. Some items were completed as part of the Process and Activities steps. The rest of the output is suitable for an enterprise-grade production implementation and is outside of the book's scope and omitted for brevity while marked with Real life in the Completed column.

Table 4-1. *Outputs and Deliverables*

Deliverable	Mandatory	Completed	Team
AWS EKS Cluster	Yes	Yes	Product Team
AWS EKS Cluster	Yes	Yes	Product Team
Virtual Private Cloud	Yes	Yes	Product Team
Network Security Group	Yes	Yes	Product Team
AWS PostgreSQL RDS	Yes	Yes	Product Team
AWS PostgreSQL RDS backup and recovery configurations	Yes	Real life	Product Team
AWS PostgreSQL DRS data security configurations	Yes	Real life	Product Team
Automation scripts (Ansible) to provision AWS EKE cluster	No	Real life	Product Team

Tools, Techniques and Best Practices

This section provides reference materials to support the architecture, design, configuration, and operation of the AWS EKS Cluster and the AWS PostgreSQL RDS. These materials are concerned with the *Infra* technology and services area.

The idea behind the list is that these technologies, tools, and techniques are aligned with the *cloud migration design principles* and allow the team to take full advantage of the cloud deployment model, *the cloud services model, the migration strategies, and the cloud computing characteristics.*

Table 4-2. *Tools, Techniques, Best Practices*

Best Practice, Tool or Technique	Description and Benefits
Amazon EKS Security	Shared responsibility model when using Amazon Security Service
Amazon RDS Security	Shared responsibility model when using Amazon RDS
AWS EKS Network Security	Additional software is required to provide fine-grained network security policy for containers
IAM User for RDS service and account management	Create new IAM user to work with database service <ul><li>Securely store login credentials</li><li>Only use it for service and account management</li></ul>
Environments parity	Development, testing, production, and disaster recovery environments should be identical or as close as possible to promote reusability, automation, security, and elimination of manual deployment and configuration steps
Kubecost	Kubernetes cost monitoring tool

Summary

At this point, you have provisioned the required cloud infrastructure. You configured the Amazon EKS Kubernetes cluster to deploy application components and a free-tier Amazon PostgreSQL relational database service (RDS). During the infrastructure configuration step, you created IAM roles, Virtual Private Networks (VPC), and security groups to ensure that a sufficient security perimeter was established.

In the next chapter, you see how to refactor application code for subsequent manual deployment into the cloud infrastructure and migrate the database to the AWS PostgreSQL provider-managed service.

CHAPTER 5

Migrate Software Application

History in its broadest aspect is a record of man's migrations from one environment to another.

— Ellsworth Huntington

In the previous chapter, we configured an AWS EKS cluster and provisioned an AWS PostgreSQL RDS to host sample application components and data in the cloud provider's infrastructure. After reading and following the instructions in this chapter, you should be able to accomplish the following objectives:

- Migrate application data to the AWS PostgreSQL Relational Data Service

- Migrate configurations into ConfigMap and deploy them to the Kubernetes cluster

- Package components into Docker containers and push images to DockerHub

- Generate Kubernetes YAML templates files for Deployments and Services

- Manually deploy application components with template files in the Kubernetes cluster

To address the "when" question, this step is performed after the cloud infrastructure has been provisioned. See Chapter 2, Figure 2-3, for reference.

© Taras Gleb 2021
T. Gleb, *Systematic Cloud Migration*, https://doi.org/10.1007/978-1-4842-7252-7_5

The following roles typically contribute to the activities described in this chapter: Developer, Operations Engineer, Quality Analyst, and Agile Master.

Complementary source code for this book is available on GitHub via the book's product page, located at *www.apress.com/9781484272510*. Recall that the structure of the sample application consists of the following tiers, components, and technologies:

- *Data tier*: Presented by application data in *demo-database* and supported by the PostgreSQL Database Engine

- *Business tier*: Presented by business application component *demo-application*, and built with Java Spring Boot framework

- *User interface tier*: Presented by application component *demo-web* and built with prevalent web framework and standard technologies: Angular, HTML, and CSS

We used a Docker container for virtualized runtime environments for both *demo-web* and *demo-application* components. Containers are deployed into either local **minikube** running in Docker Desktop or AWS EKS clusters for testing and execution. This solution is portable; all major cloud providers offer Kubernetes and it can be built from the ground up, depending on the infrastructure and security requirements. This approach accelerates the migration process, offers a higher degree of cloud maturity within the Dev, DevOps, Sec, and Ops Technology and Service areas, simplifies development flow, and minimizes the impact on application code. Additional benefits include:

- Ability to expose application components as services for horizontal scalability, reliability, manageability, service discovery, and load balancing.

- Automated deployment, including rollouts and rollbacks, as well as components health monitoring during upgrades.

- Self-healing (auto-admin) capabilities to address possible machine failure.

- Runtime elasticity to match workloads with underlying compute resources for cost efficiency.

- Deployment portability; components are environment and cloud-agnostic, as Docker container includes all required dependencies and can be run in any major cloud provider environment.

- Follows the tenth principle of Dev/Prod environment parity (*https://12factor.net/dev-prod-parity*); since the same Docker container can be run in local minikube cluster on the developer A machine, or in the cloud provider Kubernetes environments.

We use a progressively proficient approach to container deployments. First, we run the container directly from the command line inside the local Docker engine. It is a fast and easy way to get started, but the downside is that we don't keep the deployment state description in the code repository. To solve that problem and adhere to the IaC principle, we add YAML templates to each Kubernetes object (deployment, service, etc.) to describe and store application and infrastructure state in the code repository. The actual deployment still happens from the command line. In Chapter 8, we move to *Helm,* Kubernetes package manager for organizing YAML templates into a Helm chart for efficient, repeatable, and automated deployments and rollbacks for all the components in a single step.

Using Amazon PostgreSQL RDS follows the fourth principle of the 12-factor app, where the application accesses the database as a backing service. A backing service is any service the application consumes over the network as part of its normal operation, such as datastores (*https://12factor.net/backing-services*). Data is migrated with native PostgreSQL utilities, such as psql, pg_dump, and pg_restore. Alternative database migration options are the AWS Data Migration Service or third-party software tools. With either approach, data can be transferred directly between on-premise and *AWS RDS* instances or via *S3 bucket,* which is the preferred choice for the real-life data transfers scenarios due to size, security, network reliability, and speed. Optional bastion host VMs can be configured to satisfy security requirements. The Product team provisions AWS PostgreSQL RDS in a self-service manner, coherent with the cloud computing concept and the shared responsibility model. This approach is agile from the Product team's perspective, as the team is decoupled and has no dependency on the Platform team.

Configuration is critical to application development, because proper implementation, which is one of the architectural decomposition strategies, brings significant benefits to the software development and operations processes. Benefits include increased manageability, security, and flexibility, reduced vendor dependency, automation, and less human error. Conversely, deficiencies in configuration design and implementation can lead to production deployment human error, and increased manual effort and cost to maintain configurations, security breaches, and related financial losses and technical risks.

Application configuration data can be classified into three different types:

- Application bootstrap values.

- Runtime values for service locations, e.g., database services.

- Business configuration values.

From the architectural perspective, applications can access their configuration data in two ways:

- *Classic or environment*: Retrieve configuration data from its runtime environment or infrastructure. We can label it as a "north-south" access type, as the application has to go down the stack to access configurations.

- *Configuration as a Service*: Retrieve configuration data from another service endpoint. This approach is flexible, coherent with the "everything as a service" cloud-native principle, and provides appropriate decoupling for configurations to be protocol-, format-, infrastructure-, and vendor-agnostic. We can label this approach as an "east-west" configuration approach.

We follow a third principle of 12-factor app principle, which states "an app's config is everything that is likely to vary between deploys (staging, production, developer environments, etc.)".

Inputs

The following inputs, including infrastructure and services, are required to deploy the application components, data, and configuration into the cloud provider datacenter:

- AWS EKS Cluster

- AWS PostgreSQL RDS

- GitHub Code Repository

Processes and Activities

When we describe the example application architecture, we use a top-down approach—web, business, configurations, and data layers. The implementation will happen in the opposite direction, bottom-up, as each higher tier needs the lower tier as a dependency.

We start by migrating data-native PostgreSQL utilities—`psql,` `pg_dump` and `pg_restore`—which works well here for quick development, prototyping, and to demonstrate the concepts. Application data migration is independent from application components; however it is a runtime dependency and we need it before we deploy application components.

Next, we design and implement application configuration migration. Application components will be stored in Kubernetes objects, suitably called *ConfigMaps.* During implementation, we generate Kubernetes configurations and demonstrate how to use existing application configuration files as conversion inputs.

Finally, we package front- and backend application components into Docker containers. We build separate containers for each component, deploy to the local container repository, and test-run inside the local Docker engine. Introducing Docker containers into an application development lifecycle provides for fast and portable development, either in the developer desktop environment or the cloud provider infrastructure. Next, we add Kubernetes templates and YAML files that describe deployment and service objects for higher-level containers inside the cluster.

Prerequisites

To execute activities in this chapter, we need to install additional software on the local machine—the Docker software. It is a comprehensive development platform consisting of a Docker engine, an API, the user interface, a container repository, and a CLI to assist with easy development and deployment. Another prerequisite, called `kubectl`, should have already been installed in the previous chapter; it will be required to configure your computer to communicate with the AWS EKS cluster.

- *Docker:* See the Getting Started With Docker web resources to install Docker and its components to your local machine.

- *DockerHub:* See the Create DockerHub ID reference to create a DockerHub account. After you have created an account and logged into the DockerHub, you need to create two private repositories: *demo-application* and *demo-web-application*. Alternatively, you can clone the application components code from the book's repository and then push to your own.

- *Docker Desktop:* See the Docker Desktop resource to install software on your machine. This software for Windows and Mac machines builds and shares containerized applications; the installation will include a Docker runtime, the API, and a local Kubernetes cluster.

- *Configure kubectl:* To connect your computer to the AWS EKS cluster, update the *kubeconfig* file for your cluster. Listing 5-1 will either create a new *config* file in the *~/.kube* directory or will add the cluster's configuration to an existing one. Replace **<your-region-value>** and **<your-cluster-name>** with the appropriate cluster values.

Listing 5-1. Update Kubeconfig

```
$aws eks update-kubeconfig \
  --region <your-region-value> \
  --name <your-cluster-name>
```

To verify that the configuration was successful, check the current context for a kubectl client. The output should contain the context name value for your AWS EKS cluster, as shown in Listing 5-2.

Listing 5-2. Verify Current Context

```
$kubectl config current-context
Command output
arn:aws:eks:us-east-2:78xxxxxxx506:cluster/demo-aws-eks-cluster
```

It would be helpful to have a basic understanding of Docker and Kubernetes commands and the general flow, but this is not strictly required. This book assumes no prior knowledge of these technologies for executing the steps and provides helpful tips with commands and instructions.

Data Tier

To migrate the application data to AWS PostgreSQL RDS using pg_dump, follow these steps:

1. On your machine where the database is located, make a copy of the database by running **pg_dump -U postgres -d demo-database -f demo-backup.sql;** you will be asked for a **postgres** password. This command will run silently, without any output and create a dump file called *demo-back.sql* in the same directory the command was run. You can verify it by running the **ls** command.

2. In the AWS Console, change your database RDS instance security group to allow the source (your local) database machine to access the RDS endpoint. Add your IP to the security group to access the instance. Open the database security group in AWS and choose *Edit inbound Rules* then *Add Rule*. There is a My IP option in the dropdown menu; select that option to auto-populate the text box with your computer's public IP address in CIDR notation.

3. Restore the dump file created in the previous step on your machine to your AWS PostgreSQL database by executing the command in Listing 5-3 in the command window.

Listing 5-3. Create Output Dump File

```
psql -f demo-database.sql \
  --host demo-database.xxxrds.amazonaws.com \
  --port 5432 \
  --username postgres \
  --dbname demo_database
```

4. You will be asked for a password. After the password is accepted, the *demo-database.sql* file will be loaded into the AWS RDS database. To verify that all the data has been loaded, list databases by executing the **\l** command, then change to demo_database by running the **\c** command. Finally, execute the select statement. You can see the commands and partial outputs in Listing 5-4.

Listing 5-4. Verify Data Load

```
postgres=> \l
                     Command output
       Name      |  Owner  | Encoding |  Collate   |   Ctype    |  Access
                 |         |          |            |            |  privileges
-----------------+---------+----------+------------+------------+-----------
 demo_database  | postgres | UTF8     | en_US.UTF-8 | en_US.UTF-8 |
 ...
(5 rows)
postgres=> \c demo_database
Command output
```

You are now connected to the demo_database database as the postgres user.

```
demo_database=> select * from customer;
Command output
     id | first_name | last_name |              address              | age
    ----+------------+-----------+-----------------------------------+-----
     1 | Joe        | Dow       | 1 Main Street, Somewhere, Canada  | 50
     ....
    (1 row)
```

At this time, free-tier AWS PostgreSQL RDS is running, the application data has been migrated to the cloud, and the service is ready to accept connections from backend application components. This objective will be completed in the next step—build Docker containers and deploy application components into the Kubernetes clusters.

Business Tier

Before we deploy our business tier component into Kubernetes cluster, we need to perform a few housekeeping tasks. First, we have to determine which Kubernetes cluster will be used for deployment. There are few options available: either the local **minikube** or the AWS EKS cluster. This option is a dynamic setting and is determined by the current-context value in the Kubernetes configuration file. We can switch between target clusters, depending on whether we are testing locally or deploying to our cloud environment. Second, we need to create a Kubernetes *namespace* object that partitions the cluster into virtual clusters and provides an organizing scope for Kubernetes objects, where each object gets a unique identity within the namespace. It is often used as a logical unit of components organization, where a single *namespace* contains all the components for an application.

Select the Kubernetes Cluster

Deployment is cluster-agnostic and is determined by the Kubernetes `current-context` configuration value. Display a list of available clusters, the current cluster, and then switch to the desired cluster by running the following commands in the listings that follow. When you start a local Kubernetes environment, the kubectl context typically is `docker-desktop` or `minikube` cluster, as depicted in Listing 5-5, with the asterisk in the `docker-desktop` row. We changed the value to the AWS EKS cluster in the Prerequisite section. You can find this value in the AWS EKS web console: it is the *Cluster ARN* value that can be found under the Cluster configuration in the Details tab.

Listing 5-5. View Kubernetes Context

$kubectl config get-contexts
```
 Abbreviated command output
 CURRENT    NAME          CLUSTER                ...
arn:...aws-eks-cluster   arn:...aws-eks-cluster  ...
    *         docker-desktop      docker-desktop        ...
              minikube            minikube              ...
```

$kubectl config current-context
```
Command output
docker-desktop
```

$kubectl config use-context <your-eks-cluster-arn-name>
```
Command output
arn:aws:eks:us-east-2:785530736506:cluster/demo-aws-eks-cluster
```

Once the cluster is selected and set, we need to create a *demo* namespace to isolate our components from the `default` namespace by running the command in Listing 5-6. The Kubernetes namespace provides security boundaries and allows for logical grouping of applications or their components. To create a namespace and to verify it, run the command as displayed in Listing 5-6. Newly created namespaces will appear in the list of available namespaces.

Listing 5-6. Create a Namespace

```
$kubectl create namespace demo
Command output
namespace/demo created
```

```
$ kubectl get namespaces
Command output
NAME              STATUS    AGE
demo              Active    13s
default           Active    13d
kube-node-lease   Active    13d
kube-public       Active    13d
kube-system       Active    13d
```

With cluster organization in place, let's configure the business components.

Configure with ConfigMaps

In this section, we implement Kubernetes infrastructure configuration with the simple classic approach *(north-south)*, which provides ConfigMaps and Secrets stored in the *etcd* database in the Kubernetes cluster master node. This configuration is concerned with bootstrap or runtime values only, as it is recommended to store business configurations in the application datastore.

Alternatively, the Spring Config Server follows the Configuration as a Code (CaaC) approach. This is the so-called *east-west* approach that works with multiple sources (JDBC, Subversion, and HashiCorp Vault, or any Git repository or local filesystem) and provides HTTPS REST endpoints to serve JSON or TXT formatted resources. In essence, it is a language-agnostic, externalized configuration in a distributed system that could be run as stand-alone or as an embedded service. In addition, this example Spring Config Server can be notified of repository changes for properties reload through a Git repository webhook (GitHub, GitLab, Gitea, Gitee, Gogs, and Bitbucket are supported). In this book, we focus on Kubernetes-centric infrastructure environment configurations with reference to Spring Config Service provided in the Best Practices, Tools and Techniques section.

We start with the Spring Boot configuration *application.properties* file as the input source and convert its content into a ConfigMap, which is later deployed into the cluster. We create a ConfigMap object's YAML file by simply copying the content from Listing 5-7 into the appropriate node of the ConfigMap object.

Listing 5-7. File contents: application.properties

```
spring.datasource.driver-class-name=org.postgresql.Driver
    spring.datasource.url=jdbc:postgresql://host.docker.internal:5432/
    demo-database
    spring.datasource.username=postgres
    spring.datasource.password=********
    spring.datasource.driver=org.postgresql.Driver
    spring.jpa.properties.hibernate.dialect=org.hibernate.dialect.
    PostgreSQLDialect
```

Add the *ConfigMap.yaml* file to the root of the *demo-application* project and paste the contents in Listing 5-8 into the file. Make a note of the *metadata.name* value, as it will be used in the Deployment template. As you can see, the content of the Spring Boot configuration file is typically configured inside the *data* node.

Listing 5-8. ConfigMap.yaml File Content

```
apiVersion: v1
    data:
      application.properties: |-
        spring.datasource.driver-class-name=org.postgresql.Driver
    spring.datasource.url=jdbc:postgresql://localhost:5432/demo-database
    spring.datasource.username=postgres
    spring.datasource.password=********
    spring.datasource.driver=org.postgresql.Driver
    spring.jpa.properties.hibernate.dialect=org.hibernate.dialect.
    PostgreSQLDialect

      kind: ConfigMap
      metadata:
        name: demo-config-map
```

To make ConfigMap available to the Deployment object that contains our backend application, we mount it as a volume in the container by adding it to the *Deployment.yaml* file under the `containers` tag. See Listing 5-9 in bold. It will allow our application component to access configuration values at startup. Ensure that the value *metadata .name: demo-config-map* in the *ConfigMap.yaml* file matches the value *volumes.name .config-volume.configMap.name: demo-config-map* in the *Deployment.yaml* file.

Listing 5-9. Deployment.yaml File Contents

```
apiVersion: apps/v1
kind: Deployment
...
        containers:
          ...
            volumeMounts:
              - name: config-volume
                mountPath: /workspace/config
        volumes:
          - name: config-volume
            configMap:
              name: demo-config-map
```

To deploy a ConfigMap into the Kubernetes cluster, run the commands in Listing 5-10. These commands will create ConfigMaps in the demo namespace.

Listing 5-10. Create the ConfigMap

```
$kubectl create -f ConfigMap.yaml -n demo
Command output
configmap/demo-config-map created

$kubectl describe configmap -n demo
Command output
Name:          demo-config-map
Namespace:  S  demo
Labels:        <none>
Annotations:  <none>
```

```
Data
====
application.properties:
----
spring.datasource.driver-class-name=org.postgresql.Driver
spring.datasource.url=jdbc:postgresql://localhost:5432/demo-database
spring.datasource.username=postgres
spring.datasource.password=g1eb1970
spring.datasource.driver=org.postgresql.Driver
spring.jpa.properties.hibernate.dialect=org.hibernate.dialect.
PostgreSQLDialect
Events:  <none>
```

We will build and deploy business-tier Kubernetes Deployment and Service objects in the next section, which contains our backend business logic component. The Deployment object has a dependency and will read configuration values from the ConfigMaps mounted in the previous section.

Build Docker Container

We start by building backend component artifacts; in our case, it is a *.jar* file. This file and runtime dependencies will be packaged into a container using the Dockerfile instructions file. We store the image in the local container repository and run a test to verify that everything works as expected when we run the container.

First we build application.jar file in the */target* directory with **maven**, by executing the **mvn clean install -Dmaven.test.skip=true** command in the root directory of the project. If the build is successful, you should see a JAR file after you navigate to the target directory and execute the **ls -l** command; see Listing 5-11.

Listing 5-11. Build the .jar File

```
$mvn clean install -Dmaven.test.skip=true
$cd target/*.jar
$ls -l target/*.jar
\target$ ls -l
Command output

total 68316
-rwxrwx---+ 1 tgleb ... 69944159 demo-0.0.1-SNAPSHOT.jar
```

Next, we need to add the Dockerfile to the root of the project. This file contains instructions for the docker **build** command to create the application component container images. It starts from the base image that contains the required dependencies. For the Java Spring Boot application, the base image requires OpenJDK8 JVM, as shown in Listing 5-12.

Listing 5-12. Dockerfile File Contents

```
1 FROM openjdk:8-jdk-alpine
2 VOLUME /tmp
3 COPY target/*.jar app.jar
4 ENTRYPOINT ["java","-jar","/app.jar"]
```

We build the *bmi/demo-application:v1* image, tag it, and push it into the local container repository. To verify that the image was created successfully and stored in the local Docker container repository, execute the commands in Listing 5-13.

Listing 5-13. Docker Build Commands

```
$docker build -t bmi/demo-application:v1 .
Command output
...
Successfully built 44c86ef11659
Successfully tagged bmi/demo-application:v1

$docker image list
Command output
```

REPOSITORY	TAG	IMAGE ID	CREATED	SIZE
bmi/demo-application	v1	44xx9	2 months ago	144MB

Having a container image in the local Docker repository is not sufficient for AWS EKS deployment; we need to push the image into the DockerHub container repository provisioned in the Prerequisite section. Listing 5-14 establishes connection with DockerHub, creates tags for an image in the remote repository, and pushes the tagged images to it.

Listing 5-14. Docker Login Commands

```
$docker login -u docker.io/<Docker ID>
$docker image tag bmi/demo-application:v1 docker.io/<Docker ID>/demo-
application:v1
$docker push docker.io/<Docker ID>/demo-application:v1
Command output
The push refers to repository [docker.io/tgleb/bmi-demo-application]
650d44ae5212: Pushed
ceaf9e1ebef5: Pushed
9b9b7f3d56a0: Pushed
f1b5933fe4b5: Pushed
v1: digest: sha256:949f6d5f6c51f1426638ffcee989255501291efd0e079603629683ab
6c152afc size: 1159
```

Test with the Docker Engine

The testing process is fairly straightforward. The docker image can be tested either by running it inside a local Docker engine or a Kubernetes cluster. To run containers on the local docker engine and expose port 8080 to enable HTTP traffic forwarding to the container's port 8080, follow these steps.

1. Open the command window for Windows or terminal for Linux users and execute the command depicted in Listing 5-15. This command will deploy the container image from the local image repository, using the tag assigned in the build step, to the local Docker engine and will forward HTTP traffic from local host port 8080 to container port 8080. If you get an error that this container already exists, find its ID using **docker ps -a** and remove it with **docker stop** <CONTAINER_ID>. If the container starts successfully, you should see the Spring Boot application starting logo in the console.

Listing 5-15.   Docker Run Command

```
$docker run -p 8080:8080 --name demo-app -t <Docker ID> /bmi-demo-
application:v1
```
Command output

```
  .   ___            _            __ _ _
 /\\ / ___'_ __ _ _(_)_ __  __ _ \ \ \ \
( ( )\___ | '_ | '_| | '_ \/ _` | \ \ \ \
 \\/  ___)| |_)| | | | | || (_| |  ) ) ) )
  '  |____| .__|_| |_|_| |_\__, | / / / /
 =========|_|==============|___/=/_/_/_/
 :: Spring Boot ::        (v2.3.7.RELEASE)
```

```
2021-04-04 ...          : Starting DemoApplication on 9f7d342794b4with PID 1
                          (/app started by root in /)
```

2. Open another terminal for testing using the **curl** utility to access
    the application URL. If the application started successfully, you'll
    see the Spring Boot actuator JSON output in the console, by
    running the command in Listing 5-16.

Listing 5-16.   Test with the curl Command

```
$curl localhost:8080/actuator/
```
Command output
```
{
  "_links": {
    "self": {
      "href": "http://localhost:8080/actuator",
      "templated": false
    },
    "health-path": {
      "href": "http://localhost:8080/actuator/health/{*path}",
      "templated": true
    },
```

```
    "health": {
      "href": "http://localhost:8080/actuator/health",
      "templated": false
    },
    "info": {
      "href": "http://localhost:8080/actuator/info",
      "templated": false
    }
  }
}
```

3. It is a good practice to clean up the resources after testing is successful. Find the running container ID, where IMAGE ID corresponds to the value captured in the output of the **docker image list** command, and stop the container. See Listing 5-17.

Listing 5-17. Docker List Processes Command

```
  $docker ps
Command output

CONTAINER_ID  IMAGE ID              COMMAND  ...
f955b44f278b  79da37e5a3aa44xx9
  $docker stop <CONTAINER_ID>
```

Test with Local Kubernetes Cluster

4. Alternatively, you can run and test the container image inside the local Kubernetes cluster. To test images inside the local standalone **minikube** or within Docker Desktop clusters, use the equivalent **kubectl run** command. It acts as a wrapper to the Docker command.

The only difference is that we cannot make HTTP requests directly to the service inside the local Kubernetes cluster, as it is not exposed outside of the cluster's network. We need to forward HTTP traffic from the local machine to the service in the cluster. When the port forwarding is running, we can make an HTTP request using the *http://localhost:8080/actuator/* URL to test that the application is running successfully and the Spring Boot health endpoint is accessible. After executing the commands in Listing 5-18, you should see the related output, if the application started successfully.

Listing 5-18. Run the Demo in Kubernetes

```
$kubectl run demo-app --image=bmi/demo-application:v1 --port=8080.
$kubectl port-forward pod/demo-app 8080:8080
$curl localhost:8080/actuator/
Command output
{
  "_links": {
    "self": {
      "href": "http://localhost:8080/actuator",
      "templated": false
    },
    "health-path": {
      "href": "http://localhost:8080/actuator/health/{*path}",
      "templated": true
    },
    "health": {
      "href": "http://localhost:8080/actuator/health",
      "templated": false
    },
    "info": {
      "href": "http://localhost:8080/actuator/info",
      "templated": false
    }
  }
}
```

This approach provides the ability to quickly test the container inside the cluster and demonstrates the flexibility of the Kubernetes ecosystem. To production-grade deployment, we will use more advanced Kubernetes options that utilize template files to create Deployment and Services objects.

At this point, we have successfully built a `demo-application` container image and tested it, both inside the Docker engine and inside a local Kubernetes cluster.

Deploy to the Kubernetes Cluster

Running each container image in Kubernetes using the approach in the previous section is labor intensive, inefficient, and most importantly, does not take advantage of the full capabilities of the Kubernetes API and its object model. We can achieve much better results using YAML files, called *definitions, configurations, manifests,* or *templates*. This approach also follows the cloud-native Infrastructure as a Code (IaC) principle. YAML files are stored under source control, which ensures that environment deployment state matches the tagged source control configuration.

We start with a Deployment object, which describes container specification, name, and labels used by the Service Kubernetes objects for service discovery and connectivity. Let's add template files to run the image as a Deployment object exposed via Service of type Cluster IP.

Create the *Deployment.yaml* template file in the root of the project and add the contents in Listing 5-19. This object instructs Kubernetes to create or update application component instances. After the Deployment is created, the control plane will schedule instances to run on the cluster node, and the Deployment Controller will monitor those instances. If it goes down, it will be replaced with a new instance to provide a self-healing mechanism.

Listing 5-19. Deployment.yaml File Contents

```
apiVersion: apps/v1
kind: Deployment
metadata:
    name: demo-service-deployment
spec:
    selector:
      matchLabels:
        app: demo-service-deployment
    replicas: 2
    template:
        metadata:
```

```
      labels:
        app: demo-service-deployment
    spec:
      containers:
        - name: demo-service

          image: docker.io/<Docker ID>/demo-application:v1
          imagePullPolicy: ifNotPresent
          ports:
            - containerPort: 8080
          resources:
            requests:
              memory: "128Mi"
              cpu: "250m"
            limits:
              memory: "256Mi"
              cpu: "1000m"
          readinessProbe:
            httpGet:
              path: /actuator/health
              port: 8080
            initialDelaySeconds: 3
            periodSeconds: 2
            failureThreshold: 3
          livenessProbe:
            httpGet:
              path: /actuator/health
              port: 8080
            initialDelaySeconds: 5
            periodSeconds: 5
            failureThreshold: 3
          volumeMounts:
            - name: config-volume
              mountPath: /workspace/config
```

```
volumes:
  - name: config-volume
    configMap:
      name: demo-config-map
```

Add the *Service.yaml* template file to the root of the project. The file is displayed in Listing 5-20. This object implements Kubernetes networking capabilities described in the YAML template. The Service object will select and expose application containers deployed with the *label app: demo-service-deployment* and load-balance traffic across multiple pods, should you deploy ReplicaSet with more than one Deployment.

Listing 5-20. Service.yaml File Contents

```
apiVersion: v1
kind: Service
metadata:
    name: demo-service-service
spec:
    selector:
        app: demo-service-deployment
    ports:
    - protocol: TCP
      port: 8080
```

Now select the target Kubernetes cluster (local minikube, Docker Desktop, or AWS EKS) and deploy containers onto the selected cluster. Display the list of available clusters, view the current cluster, and switch to the preferred cluster by executing the proper **kubectl config** commands. The current *kubectl context* was pointing to the local cluster and had to be changed to AWS EKS. Ensure that the backend component is deployed to the same cluster and namespace where we deployed the ConfigMap; see Listing 5-21. Since we have already created a *demo namespace*, the backend Docker container image will be deployed into the same *demo* Kubernetes namespace.

Listing 5-21. View Context

$kubectl config get-contexts

```
Abbreviated command output
CURRENT        NAME            CLUSTER                    ...
arn:...aws-eks-cluster        arn:...aws-eks-cluster  ...
*       docker-desktop              docker-desktop      ...
        minikube                    minikube
```

$kubectl config use-context arn:aws:eks:us-east-2:785530736506:cluster/
demo-aws-eks-cluster

```
Command output
arn:aws:eks:us-east-2:785530736506:cluster/demo-aws-eks-cluster
```

$kubectl config current-context

```
Command output
arn:aws:eks:us-east-2:785530736506:cluster/demo-aws-eks-cluster
```

To deploy the backend image into a Kubernetes cluster and expose it to incoming traffic via the Service object, execute the commands in Listing 5-22.

Note   Notice that the namespace value demo is a command argument. Without it, the deployment will end up in the `default` namespace.

Listing 5-22. Create a Deployment Object

$kubectl create -f Deployment.yaml -n demo

```
Command output
deployment.apps/demo-service-deployment created
```

$kubectl create -f Service.yaml -n demo

```
Command output
service/demo-service-service created
```

Backend application component is deployed and exposed as a service inside the cluster. To verify object creation, run the command in Listing 5-23. In the follow-up command output, you should be able to see two pods, one cluster IP service, one deployment, and one ReplicaSet.

Listing 5-23. View All Objects

$kubectl get all -n demo
```
Command output
NAME                                  READY   STATUS            RESTARTS   AGE
pod/demo-service-deployment-...       1/1     ContainerCreating  0         74s
pod/demo-service-deployment-...       1/1     ContainerCreating  0         74s

NAME                          TYPE        CLUSTER-IP     EXTERNAL-IP
   PORT(S)     AGE
service/demo-service-service  ClusterIP   10.96.81.182   <none>
   8080/TCP    37s

NAME                                     READY   UP-TO-DATE   AVAILABLE   AGE
deployment.apps/demo-service-deployment  2/2     2            0           74s

NAME                                    DESIRED   CURRENT   READY   AGE
replicaset.apps/demo-service-deployment-...  2      2        0       74s
```

To test the service, we will run the **curl** command, which makes an HTTP call to the Spring Boot Actuator endpoint. Because at this point service is not exposed outside the Kubernetes cluster network, we have to do it in two steps (the example is for localhost, but the same approach works for the AW EKS Kubernetes cluster).

Forward the HTTP traffic from the cluster machine to the service running inside the cluster, then open another terminal and run the **curl** command. You should see the output in Listing 5-24 if the application started successfully.

Listing 5-24. Port Forward Traffic

$kubectl port-forward service/demo-service-service 8080:8080
$http://<NODE_IP_ADDRESS>:8080/actuator
$curl <NODE_IP_ADDRESS>:8080/actuator/
```
Command output
{
  "_links": {
    "self": {
      "href": "http:// <NODE_IP_ADDRESS>:8080/actuator",
      "templated": false
    },
```

```
    "health-path": {
      "href": "http:// <NODE_IP_ADDRESS>:8080/actuator/health/{*path}",
      "templated": true
    },
    "health": {
      "href": "http://<NODE_IP_ADDRESS>:8080/actuator/health",
      "templated": false
    },
    "info": {
      "href": "http://<NODE_IP_ADDRESS>:8080/actuator/info",
      "templated": false
    }
  }
}
```

Make sure to stop **port-forward** to the complete testing. You can also clean up by deleting all the objects from the *demo* namespace in the **minikube** or AWS EKS cluster. Alternatively, you can leave it running and continue experimenting with the application, as depicted in Listing 5-25.

Listing 5-25. Clean Up the Kubernetes Resources

```
$kubectl delete all --all --namespace=demo
Command output
pod "demo-service-deployment-6456cdd697-fj9kt" deleted
pod "demo-service-deployment-6456cdd697-wg4mq" deleted
service "demo-service-service" deleted
```

With a backend application component demo-application packaged and tested for Kubernetes deployment, we can move to the frontend component.

User Interface Tier
Build the Docker Container

The steps, instructions, and commands to containerize the frontend application component for Kubernetes cluster deployment are very similar to the backend component steps. The differences will address dependencies, which we denote in the Docker file, and how we compile and build component artifacts.

The first step is to compile and build Angular applications. Navigate to the root folder of the project and execute the command in Listing 5-26 to generate the compiled project files in the */dist/angular-httpclient* directory. This is required as input for the Docker image creation step.

Listing 5-26. Build Frontend Project

```
$ng build --prod
Abbreviated command output

Generating ES5 bundles for differential loading...
ES5 bundle generation complete.

...
...
Date: 2021-04-05T01:11:38.717Z - Hash: cff1bc3b5b3f67b8a9af -
Time: 75568ms
```

In order to build Docker container images that include *demo-web* build artifacts, we need to add Dockerfile to the root of the project and copy-paste the contents from Listing 5-27.

Listing 5-27. Dockerfile File Contents

```
Dockerfile
    FROM nginx:1.17.1-alpine
    COPY nginx.conf /etc/nginx/nginx.conf
    COPY /dist/angular-httpclient /usr/share/nginx/html
```

Next, we execute the docker **build** command, tag the image, and push it to the local Docker container repository. The commands to execute the steps and related outputs are depicted in Listing 5-28.

Listing 5-28. Docker Build Command

```
$docker build -t bmi/demo-web-application:v1 .
Abbreviated command output
Sending build context to Docker daemon  427.9MB
Step 1/3 : FROM nginx:1.17.1-alpine
 ---> ea1193fd3dde
Step 2/3 : COPY nginx.conf /etc/nginx/nginx.conf
 ---> deb17e91b2b2
Step 3/3 : COPY /dist/angular-httpclient /usr/share/nginx/html
 ---> a0802a80e994
Successfully built a0802a80e994
Successfully tagged bmi/demo-web-application:v1 v1

$docker image list
Abbreviated command output
REPOSITORY               TAG         IMAGE ID     CREATED SIZE
bmi/demo-web-application    v1  8c1bf119cff5 ...        144MB
```

Having a container image in the local Docker repository is not adequate for AWS EKS deployment, so we also push the image into the remote DockerHub repository. Commands in Listing 5-29 establish connection with DockerHub, create tags for an image in the remote repository, and push the tagged image to remote.

Listing 5-29. Docker Login Command

```
$docker login -u docker.io/<Docker ID>
$docker image tag bmi/demo-web-application:v1 docker.io/<Docker ID>/demo-web-application:v1
$docker push <Docker ID>/demo-web-application:v1
Command output
The push refers to repository [docker.io/<Docker ID>/demo-web-application]
9f9d9be36148: Pushed
b189c0fc2c25: Pushed
```

```
fbe0fc9bcf95: Mounted from library/nginx
f1b5933fe4b5: Mounted from <Docker ID>/demo-application
v1: digest: sha256:7933d7d1544dc54d0916951751d86fda8c68a2800c66264b759f0120
eb7b1ea9 size: 1156
```

Test with the Docker Engine

Container testing for the frontend is identical to the backend component. We can test the component container images either by running containers inside the Docker engine or the local Kubernetes cluster. To run the container inside the local Docker engine, execute the **docker run** command, then open another terminal to test by running the **curl** command. The output should be the content of the web page, which is too large to be pasted here. All commands and related output are provided in Listing 5-30.

Listing 5-30. Docker Run Command

```
$docker run --name demo-web-application -d -p 4200:80 bmi/demo-web-
application:v1
$curl localhost:4200
```

It is a good practice to clean up the resources after testing is successful. Find the running container ID, where IMAGE ID will correspond to the value captured in the output of the **docker image list** command, and stop the container, as displayed in Listing 5-31.

Listing 5-31. Docker List and Stop Process

```
$docker ps
 $docker stop <CONTAINER_ID>
```

We have built a *demo-web* container image and tested it inside the Docker engine, which runs locally on the developer's machine. Having a container ready in the container repository allows us to use a reference to that container inside the Kubernetes template files for a more advanced deployment approach, where we can keep the files and application state inside the application code repository.

Deploy to the Kubernetes Cluster

As with our backend container image, deploying images directly to Kubernetes is inefficient and does not take advantage of the full capabilities of Kubernetes API. Let's add template files to run our image as a Deployment object exposed via the Service interface of default type Cluster IP. Add the *Deployment.yaml* template file to the root of wwwell as the number of pods to start in the `replicas` field. The Service object in the next template file will select the Deployment pods for HTTP traffic forwarding inside the cluster, using the `matchLabels` field value: `app: demo-web-deployment`.

Listing 5-32. Deployment.yaml File Contents

```
apiVersion: apps/v1
kind: Deployment
metadata:
    name: demo-web-deployment
spec:
    selector:
      matchLabels:
        app: demo-web-deployment
    replicas: 2
    template:
        metadata:
          labels: deployment
            app: demo-web-deployment
        spec:
          containers:
            - name: demo-web
              image: docker.io/<Docker ID>/demo-web-application:v1

              imagePullPolicy: IfNotPresent
              ports:
                - containerPort: 80
```

Add the *Service.yaml* template file to the root of the project; see Listing 5-33. This file represents a minimalistic Service configuration. Kubernetes controllers will instantiate the default ClusterIP Service object and forward the internal HTTP traffic to port: 4200, where the *demo-web* application is listening.

Listing 5-33. Service.yaml File Contents

```
apiVersion: v1
kind: Service
metadata:
    name: demo-web-service
spec:
    selector:
        app: demo-web-deployment
    ports:
    - protocol: TCP
      port: 4200
```

We are ready to select and deploy a *demo-web* component container to the Kubernetes cluster. Deployment is cluster-agnostic and is determined by the current context configuration value. Display the list of available clusters, current clusters, and then switch to the desired cluster by running the commands in Listing 5-34. In the output, *the kubectl context* was pointing to the local cluster and had to be changed to AWS EKS.

Listing 5-34. List the Kubernetes Context

$kubectl config get-contexts

```
Abbreviated command output
  CURRENT      NAME           CLUSTER         AUTHINFO   NAMESPACE
arn:...aws-eks-cluster   arn:...aws-eks-cluster    arn:...aws-eks-cluster
     *         docker-desktop   docker-desktop     docker-desktop
               minikube         minikube           minikube
```
$kubectl config current-context
```
Command output
docker-desktop
```

$kubectl config current-context

```
Command output
arn:aws:eks:us-east-2:785530736506:cluster/demo-aws-eks-cluster
```

At this time, we have already created a *demo* namespace and the frontend image will be deployed into the same namespace as our back-end component. Deployment to the Kubernetes cluster is now much more efficient. To deploy and expose the user interface component, execute the commands in Listing 5-35. All commands should be executed from the root directory of the *demo-web* project.

Listing 5-35. Create the Deployment Object

$kubectl create -f Deployment.yaml -n demo.

```
Command output
deployment.apps/demo-web-deployment created
```

$kubectl create -f Service.yaml -n demo.

```
Command output
service/demo-service-service created
```

The application is deployed and exposed as a service inside the cluster as a default ClusterIP object. Web applications can be exposed to external access via the NodePort or IngressController Kubernetes networking objects for complete production-grade capabilities. We can see all the Kubernetes objects inside the demo namespace after executing the command in Listing 5-36. There are two ReplicaSets deployments for front-end and back-end application, each responsible for two Pods, where each deployment is exposed via Service object of type ClusterIP.

Listing 5-36. Display All Resources

$kubectl get all -n demo

```
Abbreviated command output
```

NAME	READY	STATUS	RESTARTS	AGE
pod/demo-service-deployment-667bc47f65-6nfng	1/1	Running	291	27h
pod/demo-service-deployment-667bc47f65-pd2xx	1/1	Running	291	27h
pod/demo-web-deployment-9bc778988-72s5l	1/1	Running	0	6s
pod/demo-web-deployment-9bc778988-sncks	1/1	Running	0	6s

```
NAME                                    TYPE         CLUSTER-IP      EXTERNAL-IP   PORT(S)      AGE
service/demo-web-service                ClusterIP    10.98.175.159   <none>        4200/TCP     3s

NAME                                          READY   UP-TO-DATE   AVAILABLE   AGE
deployment.apps/demo-service-deployment       1/2     2            1           27h
deployment.apps/demo-web-deployment           0/2     2            0           6s

NAME                                                DESIRED   CURRENT   READY   AGE
replicaset.apps/demo-service-deployment-667bc47f65  2         2         1       27h
replicaset.apps/demo-web-deployment-9bc778988       2         2         0       6s
```

Clean up by deleting the resources from demo namespace in the local development *minikube* or in the AWS EKS Kubernetes cluster. Execute the command in Listing 5-37.

Listing 5-37. Clean Up Kubernetes Resources

```
$kubectl delete all --all --namespace=demo
Command output
pod "demo-web-deployment-6456cdd697-fj9kt" deleted
pod "demo-web-deployment-6456cdd697-wg4mq" deleted
service "demo-web-service" deleted
```

We have prepared application components for the AWS EKS Kubernetes cluster and completed the deployment. Packaging application components into Docker containers and adding Kubernetes templates is a groundwork step for building automated pipelines in the next chapter. We will use the Kubernetes package manager *Helm,* where application build, container packaging, and Kubernetes deployment steps are executed via an automated CICD GitLab pipeline. Next, we look at the application configurations (services and integration).

Output and Deliverables

Table 5-1 provides list of deliverables required to migrate application components and data to the cloud provider infrastructure. Some items were completed as part of Process and Activities steps. The rest of the outputs in the table are suitable for an enterprise-grade production implementation and so are outside of the book's scope and omitted for brevity.

Table 5-1. *Outputs and Deliverables*

Deliverable	Mandatory	Completed	Team
Frontend component Docker image	Yes	Yes	Product team
Backend component Docker image	Yes	Yes	Product team
Deployment.yaml, Service.yaml, ConfigMap.yaml: template files for user interface and backend component	Yes	Yes	Product team
Database SSL connectivity	Yes	Real life	Product team
Ingress controller	Yes	Real life	Product team
Load balancer	Yes	Real life	Product team
SSL certificate	Yes	Real life	Product team
Kubernetes secrets for database login credentials	Yes	Real life	Product team

Tools, Techniques and Best Practices

This section provides reference materials for application code and data migration to cloud-native, cost-efficient solutions (in the Dev technology and services area). The idea behind the list is that these technologies, tools, and techniques are aligned with the cloud migration *design principles* and allow the team to take full advantage of the *cloud deployment model, the cloud services model, the migration strategies, and the cloud computing characteristics.*

Most applications were designed and built during the pre-cloud era. Developers did not give much thought or consideration to how efficient the algorithms were, how much compute resources a particular block of code consumed, or whether the collection being processed inside the loop sent an ever-increasing array list over the network. All that has changed. Today, providers introduced savvy pricing models and added pricing parameters to the API calls.

In light of those changes, we need to reevaluate application code, configuration, frameworks, and data to optimize applications for the cloud at a "line-of-code" level. Only then will the organization be able to achieve full benefits in terms of optimized resource utilization and cost-efficient solutions. One such example in the context of the sample application is replacing Spring Boot with the Micronaut (*https://micronaut.io/*) framework. It is cloud-native framework that reduces memory footprint and application startup time, which all are welcomed changes for the Kubernetes and cloud environment. This framework is designed with cloud efficiency in mind, as opposed to Spring Boot, with a reflection-based model that loads and caches reflection data for all the beans in the application context.

Development teams are no longer restricted by old deployment models where there had to be an application server as a runtime container. In addition to Kubernetes, cloud providers offer *cloud functions* or *lambdas,* where blocks of code can be executed without a server or dependency. Granted, each progressively cloud-native deployment model introduces coordination and maintenance complexity, as there is always a trade-off.

Application data is no longer constrained to RDBMS and SQL databases. Proliferation of various types of NoSQL databases allows matching data engines to data type and workload patterns. New data processing engines have been designed and built with efficiency in mind. Processing and storage are being isolated to make it easier for teams to choose a service that's optimized for processing or storage, compresses the data, and distributed and resource-efficient from the ground up.

Best practices for cloud-native application configurations start with the Configuration as a Code (CaaC) layer. This technique works well with cloud delivery models. It allows applications to reload new configuration without downtime. It also prevents configurations being deployed to some random VMs in some unknown locations, which is always a security concern.

To sum up, the best practices, tools, and techniques must be constantly reviewed and reevaluated in each application tier. This approach will allow for the application code, data, configurations, and architecture to continuously evolve and to take advantage of the cloud computing model. It will also mitigate risks, avoid common pitfalls, and problems that could jeopardize cloud migration. Table 5-2 provides some additional tools, techniques, and best practices that can provide you with pointers and ideas for future research.

Table 5-2. *Tools, Techniques, and Best Practices*

Tool, Technique, or Best Practice	Description and Benefits
AWS Database Migration Best Practices	Methodology provided by Amazon for database migration
Docker	Open-source platform for application development, deployment, and operations within virtualized environment called containers
Docker Desktop	Application for MacOS or Windows for developing containerized applications
Docker Hub	Service provided by Docker for sharing container images
Kubernetes Resource Request and Limits	Kubernetes mechanism to control CPU and memory resources
Kubernetes Readiness and Liveness Probes	Kubernetes mechanism to determine when the container is ready to accept requests and when to restart the container
Micronaut	Cloud native code
Project Loom	Lightweight Thread Management Library

Summary

In this chapter, you implemented changes to the application, data, and configurations to make the code ready for the cloud infrastructure. You also deployed applications and data to the AWS services and infrastructure, which were provisioned in Chapter 4.

Application components were packaged into Docker containers and Kubernetes template files were introduced to follow IoC principles and the cloud-native deployments methodology. Running application components in Kubernetes provides elasticity and cost-efficiency with matching workload to auto-provisioned infrastructure resources. Application components were manually deployed to the Kubernetes infrastructure to learn and better understand the moving parts of the solution.

Application data was migrated to the AWS PostgreSQL Relational Data Service. AWS provides backup, replication, and restore capabilities out of the box to allow teams to focus on business value activities, while eliminating low-level administrative tasks. The team will benefit from future innovations as new features are developed by Amazon without considerable effort from the team's side.

You are now ready to add logging, monitoring, and alerting to the application, in order to satisfy the cloud observability requirements.

CHAPTER 6

Add Monitoring, Logging and Alerting

What is not measured does not exist.

— Niels Bohr

To support successful cloud operations, we need to continuously monitor and observe the application state and its behavior in the cloud infrastructure. In Chapter 5, we deployed sample application components and data to AWS. After reading and following the instructions in this chapter, you should be able to accomplish the following objectives:

- Design, implement, and test cloud-native monitoring solutions with Prometheus and Grafana.

- Design, implement, and test cloud-native logging solutions with Elasticsearch and Kibana.

- Configure monitoring and logging for the AWS PostgreSQL RDS database.

- Provision, configure, and test the PagerDuty service for alerting, escalating, and incident management.

To address the "when" question, this step is completed after application components and data are deployed to the cloud provider infrastructure. See Figure 2-3 in Chapter 2 for reference.

The following roles typically contribute to the activities described in this chapter: Developer, Architect, Network Engineer, Infrastructure Engineer, Operations Engineer, Security Engineer, Quality Analyst, Product Owner, and Agile Master.

© Taras Gleb 2021
T. Gleb, *Systematic Cloud Migration*, https://doi.org/10.1007/978-1-4842-7252-7_6

Monitoring can be a challenging task, given that in the shared responsibility model, the team no longer has control or access to the physical datacenters, underlying virtual machines, or networking infrastructure. In this case, state and behavior can be deduced from the system's internal state and then externalized through instrumentation metrics or log events and automated alerts. Then state and behavior are provided to the Product and Platform teams. This idea originates from the *system control theory*, which is the foundation of the *feedback system*. This idea eventually resulted in an emergence of cloud-native architectural system property called *observability*. It determines how well the internal state of the system can be inferred from the externalized internal outputs. That begs the question: how do we approach externalizing the internal system state in the cloud?

When designing cloud-native monitoring, logging, and alerting solutions, we follow the same cloud computing principles as Everything as a Service (XaaS), delivered over the network in a self-serving manner. The approach isolates implementation and operation of monitoring, logging, and alerting functions between the Product and Platform teams for proper separation of concerns, and reduced dependency. This method helps improve agility, and velocity during development, migration, and operation. Monitoring, logging, and alerting services are provided by the Platform Teams and standardized across multiple Product teams without having to build and manage costly siloed solutions. Availability of AI- and ML-augmented Security Information and Event Management (SIEM) for threat detection in the observability space, introduces significant and meaningful innovations in the cloud provider environment.

Teams leverage the cloud provider infrastructure and emerging cloud-native software solutions for collection, storage, query, analysis, and backup of the logging and monitoring data. This data facilitates insights and advanced analysis as well as enhances searching and investigation capabilities. Monitoring, logging, incident alerting, and automation capabilities become external services to the applications, where any software vendor application can be simply integrated into operations. This approach adheres to Principle IV of the 12-Factor App, where applications access monitoring, logging, and alerting as a backing service. It also treats log events as external event streams, which is a Principle XI of The 12-Factor App. This design greatly reduces dependency on any particular provider and protects against the "vendor-king" architecture anti-pattern. If a service becomes too expensive or new, more advanced technology come along, teams can simply swap one for another.

This chapter looks at different degrees of cloud maturity for the monitoring, logging, and alerting solutions, and the key is to find suitable tradeoffs in the following categories:

- *Open-source vs. commercial*: To ensure cost efficiency and to apply the commercial open-source first principle.

- *High-degree of cloud maturity and vendor-neutral solutions*: To avoid vendor lock-in and to deliver cloud-agnostic solutions.

- *Best in class interoperable software*: To support innovations, AIML capabilities, and high interoperability.

- *Automation*: To reduce non-value added activities and delegate manual administrative costs to software or cloud services provider, including self-healing or auto-administration capabilities.

- *Cloud-native architecture:* To ensure proper levels of coupling, isolation, and modularity and to reduce interdependency between software components, infrastructure and IT teams.

We select, design, and implement full-stack monitoring, logging, alerting and escalation solution for the frontend, backend, and data components and the underlying infrastructure. It will be responsible for collection, aggregation, indexing, visualization, as well as search and alerting functionality. The design will provide logs and metrics for application components, database service, Kubernetes cluster, and infrastructure. The proper approach for Product teams is to design and configure application-specific sets of metrics and counters to ensure a high-degree of system observability and automation for monitoring application health. In the cloud environment, log levels should be configurable to change output without interruption to the end user, however it is still acceptable to change log setting after downtime in some scenarios. Log and metric volumes directly impact observability stack performance and accrued costs to store collected data.

Designing and implementing an automated alerting and escalation solution has to be discussed between the Product, Platform, Operations, and Business teams. We need to ensure that the solution fits well into the organization's ITSM process and is well integrated with existing procedures and is supported by software products, such as Service Now or JIRA Service Desk.

We need to carefully analyze and understand runtime and long-term storage requirements. Storage costs can easily get out of hand, and lack of storage can hinder the team's ability to conduct daily support operations with regard to observability. To put it plainly, if monitoring software hard drives has reached the storage limit, it stops working. It is recommended to determine the data retention and access policy and design different storage tiers—HOT for immediate search, WARM and COLD tiers for long-term storage.

To address the requirements and constraints described above, we present the observability solution architecture and related technology implementation stack in Figure 6-1.

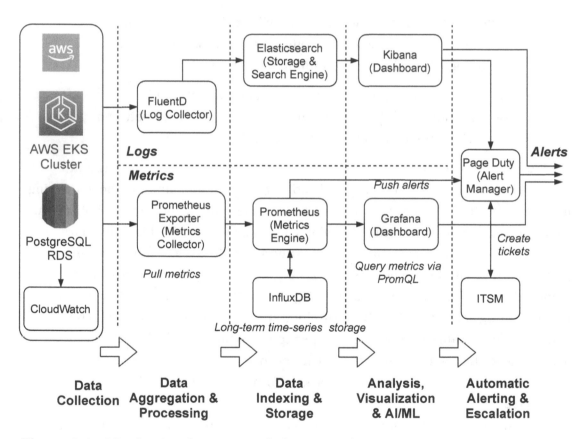

Figure 6-1. *Monitoring, logging, and alerting architecture*

The solution depicted in Figure 6-1 clearly maps the high-level steps of collection, aggregation, storage, analysis, and alerting to optimized flow of monitoring and logging data through integrated software and services.

Inputs

To build comprehensive observability support for the cloud deployment, the following inputs should be provided:

- Existing applications' monitoring and logging configurations
- AWS EKS Cluster
- AWS PostgreSQL RDS
- Application and database code in the Git repository
- Docker containers with application components
- GitHub container repository
- Current state architecture
- Future target state architecture
- Components change summary
- Risk analysis document
- Cloud resources naming and tagging
- Resource capacity and cost planning

Processes and Activities

We implement monitoring, logging, and alerting for the following application components in the list below. The frontend component is omitted from it, as the implementation is identical to the backend component.

- Application backend components: *demo-application*
- AWS EKS or Local Kubernetes cluster nodes and pods
- AWS PostgreSQL Relational Database Service: *demo-database*

We start by adding monitoring and logging capabilities to the application components, the Kubernetes cluster, and any third-party software to ensure there is full-stack monitoring and logging support. Next, we look at adding logging and monitoring capabilities to AWS PostgreSQL RDS. In addition, we will review visualization, searching, storage and finish the chapter with alerting and escalation implementation.

Prerequisites

The following software needs to be installed locally before you can continue with the activities in this chapter:

- *Helm*: See Getting Started with Helm resources at this URL: `https://helm.sh/docs/intro/quickstart/`. It would be helpful to have basic understanding of the Helm commands and general flow, but this is not strictly required. This book assumes no prior knowledge of this technology for executing the steps and provides helpful tips with commands and instructions.

- We have to provision Elastic Cloud Service in AWS cloud infrastructure. One thing to keep in mind is that Elastic Cloud services are also available in Microsoft Azure and GCP platforms, and could be configured as needed based on application target cloud provider requirements. The solutions proposed here are cloud-agnostic, and AWS is only used for convenience and egress traffic-related cost savings, since our application components and database are already running in the AWS infrastructure.

- *Elasticsearch Cloud Service (`https://www.elastic.co`)*: Cloud-based log indexing, storage, search, and visualization service.

- *Kubernetes cluster:* Local, running on **minikube** or in Amazon EKS environment. We provisioned this service in Chapter 4.

- *PagerDuty (`https://www.pagerduty.com/`)*: Cloud-based alerting service. We will add AWS, Prometheus, and Elastic Cloud Service integration when creating an account in PagerDuty SaaS.

We will proceed with minimal configurations to demonstrate the concepts and to help understand end-to-end architecture and implementation. Enterprise-grade tasks related to logs retention, backup, and replication are outside the book's scope. However, they are listed in the "Output and Deliverables" and "Tools, Techniques, and Best Practices" sections of this chapter.

Monitoring with Prometheus and Grafana

To deploy Prometheus components to Kubernetes, we use a deployment approach called Kubernetes Operator. It manages all individual components as one unit and can be downloaded from GitHub as *Prometheus Operator Helm Chart* (see *https://github. com/helm/charts/tree/master/stable/prometheus-operator*). Follow the link to review the instructions. This installation provides full-stack observability software for Kubernetes cluster, application containers, network and storage infrastructure. The end-to-end process includes data collection, storage, visualization, and out-of-the-box alerting.

First we need to add Spring Boot dependency to our backend application component to expose Prometheus metrics via the REST endpoint at /actuator/prometheus. Update the application *pom.xml* file to enable Prometheus in Spring Boot and add the dependencies shown in Listing 6-1.

Listing 6-1. Spring Actuator and Prometheus Micrometer Dependencies

```
<dependency>
    <groupId>org.springframework.boot</groupId>
    <artifactId>spring-boot-starter-actuator</artifactId>
</dependency>
<dependency>
    <groupId>io.micrometer</groupId>
    <artifactId>micrometer-core</artifactId>
</dependency>
<dependency>
    <groupId>io.micrometer</groupId>
    <artifactId>micrometer-registry-prometheus</artifactId>
</dependency>
```

Deployment with Helm commands is cluster-agnostic and target cluster is determined by the Kubernetes current-context configuration value. You can display a list of available clusters, the current cluster, and then switch to the desired one. Refer to Chapter 5 for instructions on how to navigate between different clusters. Helm has been installed locally and we can use the *prometheus-operator-helm-chart* to install Prometheus components atop Kubernetes cluster. Run **helm install** to deploy all the components, and then use the **helm list** command to verify the Prometheus Operator installation. Note that we use the same *demo* namespace for the Prometheus Operator deployment as described in Listing 6-2.

Listing 6-2. Install Prometheus Operator Components with Helm

```
$ helm install prometheus -n demo stable/prometheus-operator
Command output
The Prometheus Operator has been installed. Check its status by running:
  kubectl --namespace demo get pods -l "release=prometheus"

Visit https://github.com/coreos/prometheus-operator for instructions on how
to create & configure Alertmanager and Prometheus instances using the
Operator.
$helm list -n demo
Command output

NAME            NAMESPACE      REVISION     UPDATED
    STATUS         CHART                        APP VERSION
prometheus      demo             1           2021-04-11 12:23:14.0606759 -0400 EDT
    deployed       prometheus-operator-9.3.2    0.38.1
```

In order to visualize and query backend application metrics, locate the Grafana service in the Kubernetes cluster by running **kubectl get svc** command. Find a service named *prometheus-grafana*, and make a note of the service name and port. It should be *service/prometheus-grafana* and *80/TCP*. If you are running on a local cluster, you need to forward local HTTP traffic to the Kubernetes cluster Grafana dashboard by executing the commands in Listing 6-3. Always remember to add namespace flags to the command, as it could be a cause of frustration to not be able to find the service. Without that flag, the kubectl command is executed against the *default* namespace.

Listing 6-3. Access the Grafana Dashboard

```
$kubectl get svc -n demo
Command output
NAME                                       TYPE        CLUSTER-IP
        EXTERNAL-IP    PORT(S)                        AGE
alertmanager-operated                      ClusterIP   None
        <none>         9093/TCP,9094/TCP,9094/UDP   13m
demo-web-service                           NodePort    10.98.175.159
        <none>         4200:32290/TCP                 5d14h
prometheus-grafana                         ClusterIP   10.110.164.92
        <none>         80/TCP                         13m
$kubectl port-forward service/prometheus-grafana 80:80 -n demo
Command output

Forwarding from 127.0.0.1:80 -> 3000
Forwarding from [::1]:80 -> 3000
```

Point your browser to *http://localhost:80/* to access the local Grafana dashboard. To log in enter default user *admin* and the password *prom-operator*. After you log into Grafana, you are presented with the home screen and a default dashboard. There are many preconfigured, downloadable Grafana dashboards available on the web to fit various monitoring scenarios. We are going to use the default dashboard and monitor one of the pods from a sample application inside the Grafana dashboard. First, list the pods in the demo namespace in the console, as shown in Listing 6-4.

Listing 6-4. View Demo Service Pod

```
$kubectl get pod -n demo
Abbreviated Command Output
NAME                    READY   STATUS    RESTARTS   AGE
...
demo-service...6nfng    1/1     Running   371        6d17h
demo-service...pd2xx    1/1     Running   396        6d17h
demo-web...72s5l        1/1     Running   1          5d14h
demo-web-...sncks       1/1     Running   1          5d14h
...
```

Now we can visualize metrics for the pod; *demo-service-deployment-667bc47f65-pd2xx* in the Grafana dashboard. First, we need to open the Dashboard view by selecting the `Dashboards` menu option on the left. Once we are on the `Dashboard` page, we need to select *Datasource*: Prometheus, then `namespace:demo` and finally *pod:demo-service-deployment-667bc47f65-pd2xx* to display pod metrics, as depicted in Figure 6-2.

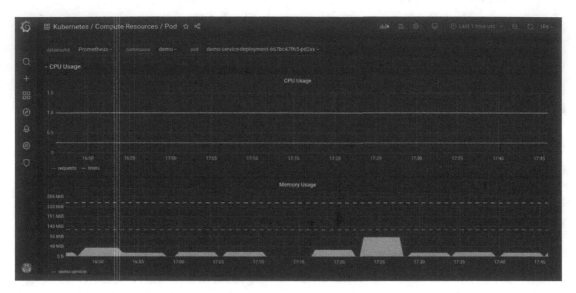

Figure 6-2. *View the pod in the Grafana dashboard*

At this point, we have installed the Prometheus Operator stack into the Kubernetes cluster and visualized the instrumentation data from nodes, pods, and application components in Grafana dashboards. Application instrumentations are exposed via Spring Boot Prometheus library and metrics are scrapped at the *actuator/prometheus REST API* endpoint.

Note   Under the shared responsibility model approach, it would typically be a Platform team that provides Prometheus and Grafana and long-term storage (e.g. InfluxDB) installation to Product teams, in order to monitor the deployment.

Logging with Elasticsearch and Kibana

Services that provide support for web, application, database, and container logs will be implemented by the EfK (Elasticsearch, FluentBit, and Kibana) software stack:

- *Fluent Bit (https://fluentbit.io/)*: Open-source log processor and forwarder that collects logging data from various sources and forwards these to a choice of destination; in our case it will be Elasticsearch.

- *Elastic Cloud Service (https://www.elastic.co)*: Full stack log aggregation, indexing, search, and visualization software.

- *Kibana (https://www.elastic.co/kibana):* Visualization software for reporting, dashboarding, and presentations.

In order to reduce application code refactoring, logging output will be redirected from log files to STDOUT. Logs for the entire stack will be collected by FluentBit and forwarded to the Elasticsearch Cloud Service created in AWS. We start with FluentBit output format configurations. To convert application components log outputs into the JSON format (other available parsers are JSON, Regex, LTSV, and Logfmt), we add the Logstash converter library dependency to the *demo-application pom.xml* file. See Listing 6-5.

Listing 6-5. Add Logstash Dependency

```
<dependency>
    <groupId>net.logstash.logback</groupId>
    <artifactId>logstash-logback-encoder</artifactId>
    <version>6.1</version>
</dependency>
```

The FluentBit pod will be deployed alongside the Pods as DaemonSet Kubernetes object, and we need to provide security configuration files that will control FluentBit access to the logging output. To achieve that, create a Kubernetes Service Account identity object for Fluent Bit pods in the *demo* namespace in the *ServiceAccount.yaml* file; see Listing 6-6.

Listing 6-6. Add Service Account Template File

```
apiVersion: v1
kind: ServiceAccount
metadata:
    name: fluent-bit
    namespace: demo
```

To install ServiceAccount inside the Kubernetes cluster, run the *kubectl create -f ServiceAccount.yaml* command inside the terminal. The *ServiceAccount.yaml* file is also available in the *demo-application* GitHub code repository. To verify successful installation, execute the **kubectl get serviceaccount -n demo** command inside the terminal, as displayed in Listing 6-7.

Listing 6-7. Install Service Account

```
$kubectl create -f ServiceAccount.yaml -n demo
Command Output
serviceaccount/fluent-bit created
$kubectl get serviceaccount -n demo
Command Output
NAME                                      SECRETS    AGE
...
fluent-bit                                1          12s
...
```

We also need to add another Kubernetes object called ClusterRole. This role will be defined in the template file named *ClusterRole.yaml*; The *ClusterRole.yaml* file is also available in the *demo-application* GitHub code repository. See Listing 6-8. This file defines the security role inside the cluster and what kind of actions it is allowed to perform. In our case, it will be actions that FluentBit pods are allowed to execute, and these actions are specified by the verbs array: get, list, and watch.

Listing 6-8. Cluster Role Template File

```
apiVersion: rbac.authorization.k8s.io/v1beta1
kind: ClusterRole
metadata:
  name: fluent-bit-read
```

```
rules:
- apiGroups: [""]
  resources:
  - namespaces
  - pods
  verbs: ["get", "list", "watch"]
```

We repeat the previous steps to create an installation by running the **kubectl create -f** *ClusterRole.yaml -n demo* command inside the terminal window. Verify the installation by executing **kubectl get clusterrole -n** *demo* inside the terminal. See Listing 6-9.

Listing 6-9. Deploy Cluster Role Template File

$kubectl create -f *ClusterRole.yaml -n demo*
Command Output
clusterrole.rbac.authorization.k8s.io/fluent-bit-read created
$kubectl get clusterrole -n *demo*
Command Output
```
NAME                                     CREATED AT
admin                                    2021-03-28T16:26:08Z
cluster-admin                            2021-03-28T16:26:07Z
edit                                     2021-03-28T16:26:08Z
```
fluent-bit-read   **2021-04-11T18:30:17Z**
...

Now we need to bind the previously added ServiceAccount and ClusterRole objects by creating a *ClusterRoleBinding.yaml* file, as depicted in Listing 6-10.

Listing 6-10. Cluster Role Binding Template File

```
apiVersion: rbac.authorization.k8s.io/v1beta1
kind: ClusterRoleBinding
metadata:
  name: fluent-bit-read
roleRef:
  apiGroup: rbac.authorization.k8s.io
  kind: ClusterRole
  name: fluent-bit-read
```

```
subjects:
- kind: ServiceAccount
  name: fluent-bit
  namespace: demo
```

Create the object by running **kubectl create -f** *ClusterRoleBinding.yaml -n demo* inside the terminal window. Verify the installation by **executing kubectl get clusterrolebinding -n** *demo* inside the command-line window, as shown in Listing 6-11.

Listing 6-11. Deploy Cluster Role Binding Template File

$kubectl create -f *ClusterRoleBinding.yaml -n demo*
```
Command Output
clusterrolebinding.rbac.authorization.k8s.io/fluent-bit-read created
```

$kubectl get clusterrolebinding -n *demo*
```
Command Output
NAME                    ROLE                            AGE
...
fluent-bit-read    ClusterRole/fluent-bit-read    39s
...
```

We also need a FluentBit ConfigMap object for the FluentBit service, which will add a Config Map for FluentBit service inside the cluster namespace, as depicted in Listing 6-12. A couple of important points to take note of:

- The path of the log files is configured with the path property in the input tag.

- The input name specifies a plug-in configured to read log files by checking the Regex in the path property and is configured as Tail.

Listing 6-12. FluentBitConfig Map Template File

```
apiVersion: v1
kind: ConfigMap
metadata:
  name: fluent-bit-config
  namespace: demo
```

```
    labels:
      k8s-app: fluent-bit
data:
  fluent-bit.conf: |
    [SERVICE]
        Flush            1
        Log_Level        info
        Daemon           off
        Parsers_File     parsers.conf
    @INCLUDE my-input.conf
    @INCLUDE filter.conf
    @INCLUDE output-elasticsearch.conf
  my-input.conf: |
    [INPUT]
        Name                tail
        Tag                 kube.*
        Path                /var/log/containers/*_container-name*.log
        Parser              docker
        DB                  /var/log/flb_kube.db
        Mem_Buf_Limit       5MB
        Skip_Long_Lines     On
        Refresh_Interval    10
  filter.conf: |
    [FILTER]
        Name kubernetes
        Match kube.*
        Kube_URL             https://kubernetes.default.svc:443
        Kube_CA_File         /var/run/secrets/kubernetes.io/serviceaccount/
                             ca.crt
        Kube_Token_File      /var/run/secrets/kubernetes.io/serviceaccount/
                             token
        Kube_Tag_Prefix      kube.var.log.containers.
        Merge_Log            On
        Merge_Log_Key        service_log
        Keep_Log             Off
```

```
        K8S-Logging.Parser   On
        K8S-Logging.Exclude Off
  output-elasticsearch.conf: |
    [OUTPUT]
        Name              es
        Match             *
        Host              ${FLUENT_ELASTICSEARCH_HOST}
        Port              ${FLUENT_ELASTICSEARCH_PORT}
        Logstash_Format On
        Logstash_Prefix log
        Replace_Dots    On
        Retry_Limit     False
  parsers.conf: |
    [PARSER]
        Name    json
        Format json
        Time_Key time
        Time_Format %d/%b/%Y:%H:%M:%S %z
    [PARSER]
        Name            docker
        Format          json
        Time_Key        time
        Time_Format %Y-%m-%dT%H:%M:%S.%L
        Time_Keep       On
```

Create the FluentBitConfigMap installation by running **kubectl create -f** *ConfigMap.yaml -n demo* inside the terminal window. Verify the installation by executing the **kubectl get configmap -n** *demo* command inside the terminal window. Find the relevant ConfigMap using its name fluent-bit-config. See Listing 6-13.

Listing 6-13. Deploy the FluentBit ConfigMap Template File

```
$kubectl create -f FluentBitConfigMap.yaml -n demo
Command Output
configmap/fluent-bit-config created
$kubectl get configmap -n demo
```

```
Command Output
NAME               ROLE                          AGE
...
fluent-bit-config Config Map/fluent-bit-config 39s
...
```

FluentBit should run on all Kubernetes nodes, which is achieved by running it as DaemonSet. Create a template file at the root of your project called *DaemonSet.yaml* and paste the contents from Listing 6-14 into the file. This file can also be downloaded from the *demo-application* GitHub repository. This template contains, among other parameters, information about the Elastic Cloud Service endpoint where logging output will be forwarded to. The environment variable name is *FLUENT_ELASTICSEARCH_HOST* and it should point to your Elasticsearch Service URL. The variable value will look similar to *https://xxx.us-east-1.aws.found.io:9243*. See Listing 6-14.

Listing 6-14. Demon Set Template File

```
apiVersion: apps/v1
kind: DaemonSet
metadata:
  name: fluent-bit
  namespace: demo
  labels:
    k8s-app: fluent-bit-logging
    version: v1
    kubernetes.io/cluster-service: "true"
spec:
  selector:
    matchLabels:
      k8s-app: fluent-bit-logging
  template:
    metadata:
      labels:
        k8s-app: fluent-bit-logging
        version: v1
        kubernetes.io/cluster-service: "true"
```

```
spec:
  containers:
  - name: fluent-bit
    image: fluent/fluent-bit:1.3.4
    imagePullPolicy: Always
    ports:
      - containerPort: 32499
    env:
    - name: FLUENT_ELASTICSEARCH_HOST
      value: "https://xxx.us-eas1.aws.found.io:9243"
    - name: FLUENT_ELASTICSEARCH_PORT
      value: "9200"
    volumeMounts:
    - name: varlog
      mountPath: /var/log
    - name: varlibdockercontainers
      mountPath: /var/lib/docker/containers
      readOnly: true
    - name: fluent-bit-config
      mountPath: /fluent-bit/etc/
  terminationGracePeriodSeconds: 10
  volumes:
  - name: varlog
    hostPath:
      path: /var/log
  - name: varlibdockercontainers
    hostPath:
      path: /var/lib/docker/containers
  - name: fluent-bit-config
    configMap:
      name: fluent-bit-config
  serviceAccountName: fluent-bit
  tolerations:
  - key: node-role.kubernetes.io/master
    operator: Exists
```

```
      effect: NoSchedule
  - operator: "Exists"
      effect: "NoExecute"
  - operator: "Exists"
              effect: "NoSchedule"
```

Create the installation by running **kubectl create -f** *DaemonSet.yaml –n demo*.
Verify the installation by executing the **kubectl get daemonset -n** *demo* command
inside the terminal window. See Listing 6-15.

Listing 6-15. Deploy the FluentBit Demon Set Template File

$kubectl create -f *DaemonSet.yaml –n demo*
```
Command Output
daemonset/fluent-bit created
```

$kubectl get daemonset -n *demo*
```
Command Output
NAME                    ROLE                            AGE
...
fluent-bit              Daemon Set/fluent-bit           39s
```

The Elasticsearch Service has been provisioned as part of the prerequisite section.
In order to show logs in Kibana, we need to configure the index pattern. *Choose
Management* then *Index Pattern* followed by *Create Index Pattern* to create the index
pattern. Next, we can select the index pattern from the *Discovery* section to view the
logs. Our *demo-application* logs are being collected by the FluentBit service that runs
on each Kubernetes node as DaemonSet, and these logs are forwarded to Elasticsearch,
where we can view them via Kibana dashboards.

Logging and Monitoring AWS RDS

In this section, we demonstrate how to utilize cloud provider logging and
monitoring service for AWS RDS SaaS. It could be a viable solution that depends on
requirements, the team's skillset, and delivery timelines. One definite advantage of this
approach is accelerated delivery capabilities, since the monitoring and logging solution
is already integrated with the database service and there is minimal administration

required. Additionally, the team can take advantage of automation, log storage configurations, and cloud provider recommendations and best practices integrated directly into the tool.

In terms of monitoring, the following metrics can be observed and stored for comparison: CPU and RAM utilization rate, network traffic, connections count, and IOps for read/writes operations. Follow these steps to provision the solution:

1. To enable AWS PostgreSQL RDS monitoring, navigate to the database console, then scroll to the *Monitoring* section.

2. Select *Enable Enhanced Monitoring* for database instances, as shown in Figure 6-3.

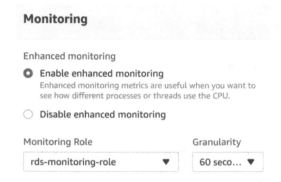

Figure 6-3. *Configure AWS PostgreSQL RDS enhanced monitoring*

3. Select the *Default* property to have RDS create a role named `rds-monitoring-role` so RDS can communicate with the CloudWatch Logs service.

4. Pick the Granularity property, which is the interval, in seconds, between points when metrics are collected. The property can be set to between 1 and 60 seconds.

To view metrics reported by this configuration, in the RDS console, navigate to *Enhanced Monitoring*; see Figure 6-4.

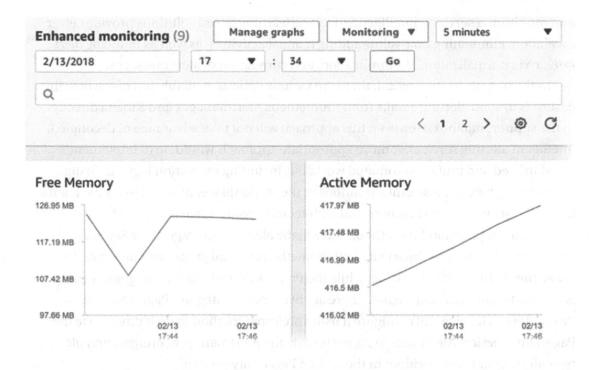

Figure 6-4. *View AWS PostgreSQL RDS enhanced monitoring*

More information about this service capability can be found on the AWS Documentation page "Using Enhanced Monitoring" at *https://docs.aws.amazon.com/ AmazonRDS/latest/UserGuide/USER_Monitoring.OS.html.* This topic is extensive and involves a deed-dive into the AWS PostgreSQL RDS set of features.

Alerting and Escalation via PagerDuty

Modern IT environments represent layers upon layers of disparate monitoring and alerting software; they generate hundreds if not thousands messages that lead to *white noise* and *alert fatigue,* while missing critical problems. Cloud migration presents an opportunity to rethink, redesign, and reimplement these systems in the context of cloud computing models.

Following the everything as a service paradigm, reflected both in the 12-Factor Methodology and cloud computing characteristics, we should look at isolating alerting functions into specialized services, plugged into and extending application logging and monitoring services. Intelligent, machine learning based solutions provide clever escalation, eliminating non-value-adding manual activities, as well as reducing *alert fatigue* via normalization, de-duplication, and correlation of alert messages.

In the migration application, there are various options available out of the box; the easiest is to send alerting emails from Prometheus Alertmanager and Kibana directly to the support mailbox. However, this approach will not take advantage of decoupled, intelligent alerting services. A more appropriate approach would be to implement standardized and unified automated workflow, including escalation logic, utilizing PagerDuty. There are also other solutions in the marketplace, depending on the team's migration scenarios and business and architecture requirements.

To send application Prometheus and Kibana alerts to the PagerDuty Service, follow steps below. The PagerDuty and Prometheus official guides can be located at *Prometheus Integration Guide*, while the PagerDuty and Kibana integration guide is at *Kibana Integration Guide*. There are two ways to integrate PagerDuty and Prometheus. Here we will configure it using preferred method to do it directly via the PagerDuty service. Alerts sent to PagerDuty via the Alertmanager configuration file typically trigger a new incident in the related PagerDuty service.

1. On the PagerDuty dashboard *Services* menu, select **Service Directory**.

2. Next, enter a name and a description for the service. Select *Integration Type* to be configured. For more details, see the "Create a New Service" documentation section.

3. Once you are redirected to the *Integration* page, select and copy the Integration Key for the later steps.

4. Create the Prometheus Alertmanager configuration file. For an example, see *https://github.com/prometheus/alertmanager/ blob/master/doc/examples/simple.yml*.

5. Create a receiver for PagerDuty in your configuration file, as follows.

```
receivers:
- name: YOUR-RECEIVER-NAME
  pagerduty_configs:
  - service_key: YOUR-INTEGRATION-KEY
```

6. Next, configure the default route to send alerts that don't match existing custom routes to the PagerDuty receiver.

```
route:
  group_by: [cluster]
  receiver: YOUR-RECEIVER-NAME
```

7. It is also possible to configure custom routes to send alerts to different receivers based on different matching conditions. See the following code snippet. In essence, different receivers could be configured with various integration keys and different routes.

```
route:
    match:
      severity: 'warning'
    receiver: YOUR-RECEIVER-NAME
```

8. Restart *Alertmanager* for the configuration changes to take effect.

Once these steps are completed, the Prometheus Operator installation and configuration on the local Kubernetes or in the AWS EKS cluster is completed with regard to monitoring and alerting capabilities. Alerts will be sent to PagerDuty for automated alerting, escalation, and incident management.

Output and Deliverables

This section lists deliverables that support the cloud deployment observability capability. We indicate which deliverable is implemented as part of this book, and which ones are more suitable for enterprise-grade production implementation. In addition, we arbitrarily assign each deliverable to either the Product or Platform team, as each IT environment is very distinct and lines of responsibilities can be drawn differently. See Table 6-1.

Table 6-1. *Outputs and Deliverables*

Deliverable	Mandatory	Completed	Team
Prometheus Operator to provision Prometheus and Grafana components Kubernetes cluster	Yes	Yes	Platform/Product team
Elastic Cloud Service is provisioned in the cloud	Yes	Yes	Platform team
Application code refactored to expose logs to Elasticsearch via standard interfaces	Yes	Yes	Product team
Access granted to visualization tools: Kibana and Grafana	Yes	Real life	Platform team
Application specific metrics added to code	Yes	Real life	Product team
Monitoring and alerting template to document alerting and escalation flow for implementations	Yes	Real life	Product team
Custom Grafana Dashboards	Yes	Real life	Product team
Alerting rules are defined using Prometheus alerting language for application alerts and escalation	Yes	Real life	Product team
Long-term metrics storage provisioned and configured	Yes	Real life	Platform team
Alert escalation policies and plan that specifies who gets alerts and how alerts get escalated	Yes	Real life	Product, Platform, and Operations teams
Monitoring and logging compute (vCPU), RAM (GB) storage (GB) for Hot, Warm, Cold requirements have been determined, documented, and implemented; including retention, migration between storage tiers, and deletion policy	Yes	Real life	Product, Platform, and Operations teams
Prometheus Operator Alertmanager and PagerDuty are integrated (Platform and Product teams, completed here)	Yes	Yes	Platform/Product team
Elasticsearch Kibana and PagerDuty are integrated	Yes	Yes	Platform/Product team

(continued)

Table 6-1. (*continued*)

Deliverable	Mandatory	Completed	Team
Monitoring database using PostgreSQL Prometheus exporter (only if using Kubernetes based database deployment)	Yes	Real life	Platform/Product team
Influx DB for long-term metrics storage	No	Real life	Platform/Product team

Tools, Techniques and Best Practices

This section provides reference materials to cloud-native, cost-efficient *monitoring, logging, and alerting solutions* (in the Ops technology and services area). The idea behind the list is that these technologies, tools, and techniques are aligned with the *cloud migration design principles* and allow the team to take full advantage of the cloud *deployment model, the cloud services model, the migration strategies, and the cloud computing characteristics.*

The ultimate objective for the monitoring, logging, and alerting solution is to help the Product and Platform teams achieve application operational stability, high-performance, and quality within the cloud provider infrastructure. One of the substantial cultural changes for the IT teams is to realize that you are no longer in the private datacenter, where you are in full control of the quality of your computing and networking gear or level of experience for your administrative resources. You are dealing with commodity computing and have to mitigate all the risks and unknowns that could emerge as a result.

A migration to the cloud provider infrastructure brings about a paradigm change to the way we monitor our applications. We need to have secure, real-time visibility, or *observability* into cloud deployments, which includes application components, data, and infrastructure. Tools provide metrics and logs for visual analysis, measurement, and accelerated automated response. This list of capabilities in the cloud would be incomplete without self-healing and automated, machine-learning-based response, which could be built into the system's reaction loop.

To mitigate the possible negative impact of Conway's Law, you have to clearly define the responsibilities within Product and Platform teams for proper coupling and isolation of the services and software. If done right, the proper separation of concerns will lead to high-productivity, agility, velocity, and reduced frictions. Unfortunately, the opposite is also true.

It is important to incorporate cloud-native, open-source technologies for cloud-agnostic and cost-efficient solutions. Tools that collect, aggregate, and forward metrics for example can range from the extremely efficient FluentBit, which is only 450KB in size, to resource-hungry commercial offerings. Teams need to have crystal-clear definitions of which metrics are important and relevant before implementation into production to reduce noise, metric fatigue, and storage cost. A generic good example of such relevant requirement is "response time for critical business function."

Similar concerns should be applied to application logs. The team should ask a set of questions before implementing the solution: what is the appropriate log configuration level for normal operations and what level is needed to investigate and perform efficient root cause analysis? Log configurations should be dynamic and allow for change without application restarts. Log data in itself does not provide much value, hence cost-benefit analysis should be performed when logging storage retention period is discussed.

Teams should automate reporting for specific metrics, e.g., Mean Time to Recover (MTTR) to measure how long it takes to identify, investigate, and resolve application issues. This metric will help evaluate the tool stack efficiency and relevancy

To sum up, best practices, tools, and techniques must be constantly reviewed and reevaluated in each step of cloud-native observability. This approach allows for the application code, data, and configurations to be continuously monitored and to take advantage of the self-healing and automated response capabilities. It will also mitigate risks and avoid common pitfalls and problems that could jeopardize cloud migration. Table 6-2 provides some additional tools, techniques, and best practices that provide you with pointers and ideas on future research.

Table 6-2. *Tools, Techniques, and Best Practices*

Tool, Technique, or Best Practice	Description/Benefits
AIOPs	Application of artificial intelligence (AI), to collect, aggregate, and analyze large volumes of application, infrastructure metrics, logs; identify significant events and either provide actionable insights or automatically resolve issues without human interventions
Adjustable and dynamically configurable log levels	Design for logging configuration that allows for dynamic configurations for an efficient approach to logging volume and details outputs
Dynatrace	Monitoring platform to monitor application, databases, and infrastructure performance
Logs and Metrics Transmission Best Practice	Use configuration management system for deployment of logging configurations, filter sensitive data, use fault-tolerant protocols, retry if sending fails, encrypt sensitive data in transit
Logs and Metrics Collection Frameworks Best Practice	Use standard, easily configurable logging frameworks that have flexible output options, standard format (JSON), and schema, avoid vendor lock-in across all your teams
Logs and Metrics Management Best Practice	Implement efficient TCO solution; compute, storage, bandwidth, compaction capabilities all should be taken into consideration
New Relic	Observability platform to collect and analyze instrumentation, metrics, logs, and other data to understand and improve systems under observation
RED Observability Method	Request Rate, Errors, Duration key metrics and observability methods
Splunk Suite of Tools	Observability solution used for application management, operations, and compliance
USE Observability Method	Utilization, saturation, and errors method for implementing observability

Summary

In this chapter, we implemented monitoring, logging, and alerting solutions to provide full-stack, cloud-native observability capability for the application components, database and infrastructure in the cloud provider data center.

We collected application and infrastructure metrics with Prometheus, then displayed them using the Grafana dashboard for monitoring, visualizing, and querying application state, including the underlying Kubernetes infrastructure. Next, we processed application logs with the EfK (Elasticsearch, FluentBit, and Kibana) stack for log collection, aggregation, forwarding, visualization, querying and machine learning capabilities. PagerDuty PaaS provides automated platform for alerting and escalation capabilities to enable accelerated response and resolution to incidents in the cloud environment.

These technologies provide a high-degree of cloud maturity, are fully supported by *CNCF*, and deliver a wealth of real-time information for actionable insights into application and infrastructure state for IT teams. Decoupling metrics and logs from application code follows Principle XI of The 12-Factor App methodology. Teams can benefit from innovations in machine learning and artificial intelligence that automate response to incidents and provide self-healing capabilities.

We are now ready to move on to "Part III: Software Deliver Migration," which dives into automated, cloud-native software delivery methodology and implementation.

PART III

Software Delivery Migration

This part of the book focuses on automated, cloud-agnostic, and secure software delivery. All the chapters provide theoretical deep-dives and practical implementation steps for the software delivery technology and service area (DevSecOps). This area is fundamental and critical since it serves as a bridge or value delivery conduit between the software delivery and operations. See Figure III-1.

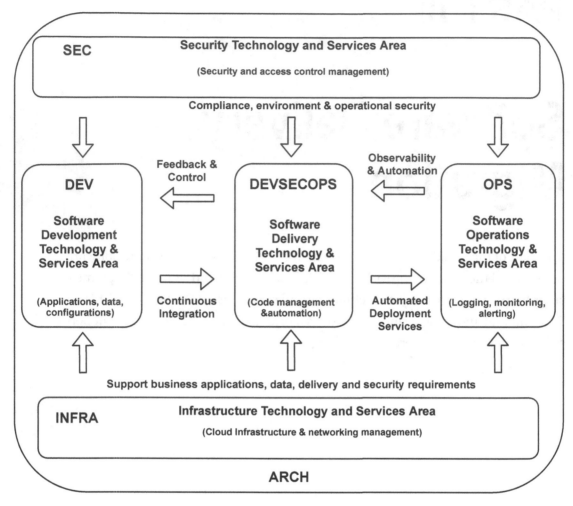

Figure III-1. *Cloud migration technology and services areas*

Software delivery migration is the last step before software operations migration. Chapter 7 introduces the cloud-native software delivery model and demonstrates how to enhance cloud migration through thoughtful integration of core organizational capabilities: *people, process, and technologies.* As you might recall from Chapter 2, successful migration implies deep synergy between each element, which also helps avoid the friction and inefficiencies identified by Conway's Law.

We propose optimized delivery flow (*processes*) consisting of problem-solving, self-managing (self-organizing), and cross-functional Product/Platform teams (*people*) that are supported by best-of-breed, cloud-native tools (*technologies*). These tools present a sound financial investment, as well as bring innovation and learning capabilities into the organization.

Software selection enables repeatable, agile delivery of quality software to help organization achieve competitive advantage via accelerated delivery of high-quality software into the cloud. Regardless of the organization type you work for, materials covered in Chapter 7 provide support for the value delivery pipeline in any industry. We conduct software delivery toolset selection within the given *business (functional)* and *architecture (non-functional)* requirements, as well as the cloud migration strategy. The software that's provisioned, configured, and integrated into the cloud-native software delivery environment consists of the following:

- *JIRA*: Workflow and organizational reporting software

- *Confluence:* Business requirements and knowledge repositories

- *GitLab*: Integrated DevOps platform for continuous integration (CI), continuous delivery (CD), and continuous deployment (CD) functionalities

Chapter 8 introduces you to the sample implementation GitLab code for the DevSecOps pipeline. Pipeline design and implementation will touch upon application, data, configuration, security, and feature management areas. The pipeline steps cover *continuous integration, continuous deployment, and continuous delivery*, and provide the ability to deploy, upgrade, roll back, and delete software releases within the provisioned cloud provider environments. Real-life scenarios typically include Dev, QA, UAT, and Prod environments, which are omitted here for brevity, since we only have a single cloud environment to work with.

Within the CICD pipeline example, there is a wealth of implementation details about various testing types. In addition to the all-familiar unit, function, integration, and performance testing, the text introduces cloud-critical *static application security testing (SAST), dynamic application security testing (DAST), containers compliance and security scanning, and open-source dependency testing.*

To have a feedback loop and control the cloud migration progress, we introduce an industry accepted set of DORA metrics—*Deployment Frequency (DF), Mean Lead Time for changes (MLT), Mean Time to Recover (MTTR), and Change Failure Rate (CFR)*—to evaluate migration progress velocity and quality.

To summarize; information covered in Chapters 7 and 8 provides solid foundational support for an organization's software value delivery pipeline.

CHAPTER 7

Procure Software Delivery Environment

You can't build a great building on a weak foundation.

— Gordon B. Hinckley

Cloud computing characteristics and service delivery models are intrinsically supportive of agile, high-velocity, and automated software delivery processes without compromising security, quality, or compliance. After reading and following the instructions in this chapter, you should be able to accomplish the following objectives:

- Develop a practical understanding of the *cloud-native software delivery model* within the DevSecOps software and technology migration area.

- Review a sample process and toolset that brings synergy between an organization's cloud migration success factors: *people, process, and technology*.

- Configure the JIRA, Confluence, and GitLab tools for a cloud-native software delivery environment.

- Present cloud-native agile development workflow within a provisioned environment.

To address the "when" question, this step is performed before we start building an automated software delivery pipeline. See Figure 2-3 in Chapter 2.

The following roles typically contribute to the activities described in this chapter: Developer, Architect, Operations Engineer, Quality Analyst, Product Owner, and Agile Master.

© Taras Gleb 2021
T. Gleb, *Systematic Cloud Migration*, https://doi.org/10.1007/978-1-4842-7252-7_7

Mandatory version control and automated pipelines increase consistency and correctness and maximize the developer's time for value-added activities. The declarative over imperative software deployment approach further reduces the manual effort required to maintain the system in a healthy state.

However, the ideal end-state that enables desired synergy between people, processes, and technologies is not a self-fulfilling prophecy. It is accomplished via thoughtful process design, organizational structure alignment, and selection of a supportive, future-proof software toolset. Then we combine these ingredients into a coherent and automated process.

Cloud migration both presents an opportunity and necessitates changes, in the way that teams deliver software, to achieve effective and efficient migration, enhance productivity, trim down waste, and eliminate non-value added activities. Every organization needs to establish essential capabilities in three core success areas: processes, people, and technologies, where all work together and in synergy with cloud computing characteristics and models to give business an edge over competitors. This synergy will inevitably allow teams to achieve high-productivity, reduce costs, and deliver high-quality software. All these objectives must be achieved while enhancing security, observability, and compliance.

We begin with the process design and then look at the people and technology aspects that sustain the process and work within it. Often it happens the other way around, where teams choose the software and then fudge the process that is either supported, if you are lucky, or constrained by the tools. In the process area, we start by establishing foundational building blocks or methodologies. We suggest agile software delivery methods, as declared by the Agile Manifesto *(https://agilemanifesto.org/)*, which has been a conventional delivery approach for the last decade. This methodology is not new, to some developers' surprise, and is rooted in *Lean* or *Toyota Production System* (TPS), invented in 1930 by Toyota's founder Sakichi Toyoda, chief engineer Taiichi Ohno and founder's son Kiichiro Toyoda. It is based on the philosophy of just-in-time, quick production of small batches of output, where quality is built-in and the team relentlessly eliminates waste and non-value added activities. Cloud-native DevSecOps builds on and extends directly from these two fundamental methodologies. A good descriptive model that adds implementation specifics would be CAMS (short for Culture, Automation, Measurement, and Sharing). Within DevSecOps we have seen emergence of new ideas and principals such as: Shift Left, Test Driven Development, Behavior Driven Development, the list goes on. All these concepts are supported by software and tooling within the DevSecOps ecosystem.

Lean manufacturing and agile development methodologies are implemented by empowered Product or Platform teams. To benefit from cloud deployment characteristics and deployment models, these teams should be problem-solving, self-managed (self-organizing), and cross-functional. These kinds of teams thrive in the cloud environment. With proper coupling and isolation with regard to software dependencies, development process, and team organization boundaries, they are exceptionally agile and deliver their software with high velocity.

There are no dependencies on other teams and no bottlenecks; the team can provision its own infrastructure via cloud provider self-service capabilities. Additionally, teams can control costs, automate deployments, eliminate waste or non-value added activities, and benefit from cloud provider innovations by moving to cloud provider services. This type of organizational structure aims to mitigate the impact of Conway's Law—as processes, teams, services, and software are demarcated along the same set of lines in the *shared responsibility model.*

To support processes and teams, we select tools that satisfy the following design principles:

- Works well in an agile environment and supports the CAMS model.

- Designed and built for the cloud provider environment.

- Supports automated continuous integration, continuous delivery and continuous deployment process that encompasses infrastructure, application code, data, and security.

- Provides high-productivity environment, reduces or eliminates waste, and allows the team to focus on value-added activities: e.g. reduce unneeded email chatter during development by automatically moving workflow items between different phases.

- Teams benefit from innovations by the software tools vendors and cloud provider services.

The toolset consists of JIRA, workflow automation, Confluence, knowledge base and GitLab, and an integrated DevSecOps platform for automated continuous integration, continuous delivery and continuous deployment. Figure 7-1 provides a unified view of *people, processes, and technologies* that support our automated pipeline, which will be implemented in the next chapter.

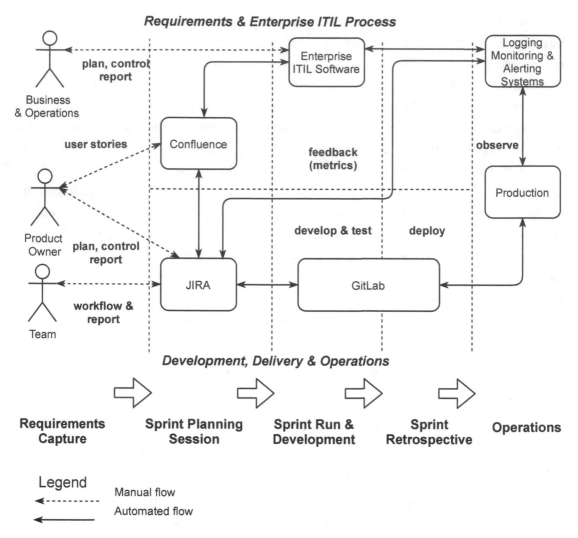

Figure 7-1. *Processes, people, and technology flow*

Note   It is worth noting the importance of the automated feedback loop that completes the cycle and flows into the development, business, IT management, and operations teams. It leads to full process visibility, early identification of issues, and the ability to apply corrective actions as required.

Software tools implemented in this chapter represent the best-of-breed solutions to satisfy requirements and selection criteria. However, in our case we have a limited set of requirements, whereas real-life scenarios can warrant different tools at the end. One such example requirement, from personal experience, was the need to avoid breaking the team's build server when a single developer pushed the latest changes. The team was large, and if someone pushed changes that broke the build on the server, everyone else was blocked for the rest of the day from pushing changes, or in the local development due to broken local build after updating from repository. The solution was to deploy *IntelliJ TeamCity*, which provides a remote build function, where local changes are compiled against the latest repository branch in isolated manner. The build failures would only be virtual and displayed to the developer who was attempting to push changes without affecting the rest of the team.

Inputs

The following inputs from the previous chapters, or from outside of this text, are required to design the automated continuous integration and delivery process, and to select and provision the necessary software tools and services:

- Application code in the Git Repository

- Database code in the Git Repository

- Application delivery process

- Database delivery process

- Application deployment scripts

- Database deployment scripts

- Application security configurations

- Database security configurations

- Current state architecture

- Future target state architecture

- Risk analysis document

This inventory provides a basic set of inputs in the context of the generic cloud migration process and our sample application. The list could be adopted and extended with organization specific artifacts, documents, and policies in mind. After we collect the necessary inputs, we can move on to the process and activities.

Processes and Activities

Activities conducted here will build an integrated environment for cloud-native, agile DevSecOps processes and an automated pipeline. We provision, configure, and integrate a set of software and services that seamlessly work together for end-to-end automated software development and delivery. Gone are the days when the development team had to install and maintain local installation of tools, such as JIRA or code repository. It is worth noting, though, that some large enterprises still maintain in-house installation for security or regulatory reasons.

Smaller organizations with limited IT resources use web-based services, where service providers take over the service administration. Following the *everything-as-a-service* principle, where we use SaaS tools, the following tasks in this chapter are non-programmatic but rather configurations and orchestration. For the instructions, you are directed to the particular service provider documentation pages to follow the steps. There is no need or value to replicate these instructions in the text for two reasons—these instructions already exist on the page and the service provider's pages are always up to date.

Prerequisites

There are no prerequisites for this section for local tool installation, as all the software is cloud-based. The only requirement is to have a stable Internet connection.

Atlassian JIRA Configuration

JIRA is one of the products offered by Atlassian, and it is designed to assist teams manage workflow for a full software development lifecycle (SDLC). Teams can plan user themes, initiatives, epics, stories, issues, and sprints; they can assign tasks to team members for implementation, and then collaborate and track execution progress. In addition, the tool provides support for release management by extended reporting capabilities that help report and improve team performance based on real-time metrics collection.

To configure JIRA and its components, we will use the Atlassian JIRA Service (*https://www.atlassian.com/software/jira*). Other options include a datacenter or configuring an on-premise server, which is outside of the scope of this book. In terms of the cloud deployment, there are various pricing plans available to choose from. There are free-trial and free-tier options for small teams. You can pick the option that suits you best, and it is always possible to change it later.

1. Navigate to *https://www.atlassian.com/software/jira* and follow steps to create a team account.

2. After the *JIRA* account is created, start with the first project using the "Getting Started" documentation page at *https://www.atlassian.com/software/jira/guides/getting-started/basics*.

Once you have JIRA service provisioned and configured, you are ready to move on to adding Confluence as a knowledge base and content management system to support JIRA workflows.

Atlassian Confluence Configuration

Confluence helps create and manage project-related information in a single workspace. Given that we live in a knowledge-based economy, and building a learning organization is one of the critical supplementary tasks of cloud migration, Confluence becomes a vital tool to store institutional knowledge and provide convenient access to the information. Interoperability with JIRA helps connect information, e.g., software requirements from Confluence to software implementation tasks captured in JIRA.

Confluence is a great collaboration and productivity tool. One real-life example is where requirements in Confluence were updated by the external customers directly, skipping the sometimes broken phone of the requirements elicitation sessions, and the development team had immediate access to the latest information, while building the software and designing their test cases. This approach cuts out the middleman, reduces email clutter, and provides a clear line of sight between requirements entered by the actual user, developer, and final delivered software version. It improved output, reduced non-value added activities, such as reading emails, which is one of the black holes of corporate productivity, as well as increased software delivery velocity and enhanced software quality.

To configure Confluence use the Atlassian Confluence Service web page (*https://www.atlassian.com/software/jira*). Once again, we are going to provision and configure a cloud-based instance.

1. Navigate to *https://www.atlassian.com/software/confluence* and follow steps to create a team account.

2. After the Confluence account is created, start with the first project using the "Getting Started" documentation page.

3. There is no need to perform the steps to connect JIRA and Confluence, as this integration comes out of the box. This integration was not available a couple of years ago for on-premise installation, which again proves the advantages of the SaaS delivery model.

We have provisioned workflow, productivity, and collaboration, and the knowledge toolset and are ready to add the DevSecOps platform for designing and implementing the software delivery pipeline.

GitLab Configuration

GitLab is a unified, end-to-end DevSecOps platform that builds and delivers software code in a manner that is fully supportive of the Agile delivery methodology. It provides that highly sought after synergy between people, processes, and technologies, where there is no friction between the process and the underlying integrated software toolset.

This is another paradigm shift introduced by GitLab, often lost in translation by the development teams in the endless discussions about GitLab vs. GitHub. The question is not one-versus-another as one goes over a list of features. It is possible for the GitLab platform to replace entire set of the tools: GitLab, Jenkins, Artifactory, Docker Container Repository, including secrets management software such as HashiCorp Vault. All these capabilities are built-in and available out of the box as a configuration option, as opposed to being labor-intensive integrations with third-party software. GitLab eliminates toolchain complexity, reduces administrative and monetary costs, and needs to learn, administer, and integrate, multiple tools.

The GitLab Runner component communicates with the repository server, pulls the artifacts, executes the pipeline and deploys software to the runtime environment. It can be installed virtually anywhere, from local machines to corporate datacenters to the cloud provider's Kubernetes cluster. This architecture provides boundless flexibility to on-premise, public, or hybrid cloud deployment models. This makes GitLab an excellent cloud-native, open-source tool that helps reduce cost, improve productivity, eliminate non-value administrative activities for third-party tools, and avoid the dreaded vendor lock-in design anti-pattern.

GitLab is built on top of open-source software and there are multiple ways to manage your GitLab instance. Options include configuring an on-premise server, which is a viable choice depending on the team's infrastructure, security, and other requirements. It could be provisioned as GitLab SaaS or deployed to any cloud provider infrastructure as a self-managed SaaS. Here we take a similar approach as with JIRA and Confluence, and use the second option—GitLab SaaS.

To configure GitLab, navigate to the GitLab URL (*https://about.gitlab.com/*). If the service model is selected, there are various pricing plans available to choose from. There are free-trial and free-tier options. You can pick one that suits your team best and remember, it is always possible to change it later. Follow these steps to configure the GitLab SaaS installation.

1. Navigate to *https://about.gitlab.com/* and follow the steps to create a team account.

2. After the GitLab account is created, start with the first project using the "Getting Started" documentation page.

3. To enable JIRA-to-GitLab integration for automated work tracking and reporting, navigate to the "GitLab to JIRA" integration page.

There are different ways to automate team work from GitLab to JIRA, e.g. teams can automatically detect activities between the two or integrate the code repository with *JIRA Development Panel* to access branches, commits, or merge requests directly from JIRA issues (only available in the Enterprise Edition). One example that this integration provides is so-called *smart commits*. They are an automation feature where each time the JIRA item ID is included in the **git push** command, it will change the status of that item automatically inside the JIRA item and add comments from the commit to the *JIRA Development Panel*.

GitLab is the final software in our toolset to support software delivery migration processes. This set is not absolute, final, or all-inclusive; new software and features are being released into the market all the time. However, this toolset provides a good starting integrated software suite for enhancing cooperation and productivity between people, processes, and technologies for efficient and effective software delivery migration.

Sample Agile Development Workflow

After we have configured our DevSecOps toolset, let's walk through a typical, yet very simple, software development workflow using the software tools. Imagine that we work as a developer in the IT department we had a business request to change the label value on our sample web application component. The workflow consists of the following steps:

- Add a product requirement to the Confluence to capture functionality, acceptance criteria, and other related information.

- Create the corresponding JIRA work item to track the development and link it to the Confluence page to include requirements in the work item for knowledge sharing and collaboration.

- Display commit messages from GitLab in JIRA for automated tracking of development work.

Let's start by adding product requirements to Confluence. Confluence has a special template for the product requirements with best practices of what is to be included in this type of document. To create a template, click the **Create** button and after the new page appears, put the cursor into the *Templates* text box on the right and type **Requirements** to create the corresponding template page and select it. It's that simple. Now you can add in required information, as depicted in Figure 7-2.

Requirement Number One

Created by Taras Gleb
Just a moment ago • 1 min read

Target release	1.0
Epic	Great Demo Project Epic
Document status	DRAFT
Document owner	Product Owner
Designer	Product Designer
Tech lead	Tech Lead
Technical writers	Plenty
QA	Yes

Objective

Change Label Button

Figure 7-2. *Create Confluence product requirement*

In the next step, the Product Owner will create a JIRA issue that will describe what needs to be completed. It will assign the issue to the developer or save it to the backlog. To create a new JIRA item, click the **Create** button on top of the page. This calls up a dialog page.

You must select the project to which the issue is assigned, in our case it is a *demo* project, and issue type, which is Task. Provide a quick summary. Once you have entered all the information and clicked **Create**, your item will be created and you can navigate to it; see Figure 7-3.

Create issue   Import issues   Configure fields ∨

Project*
⊞ demo (DEMO)   ∨

Issue Type*
☑ Task   ∨   ⑦

Some issue types are unavailable due to incompatible field configuration and/or workflow associations.

Summary*
Change Button Label|

Description
Style∨   B   I   U   A ∨ ᴬᴬ∨   𝒫∨ 🔲∨   ⁞☰ ☰   ▣∨ +∨   ≈

☐ Create another   **Create**   Cancel

Figure 7-3. *Create a JIRA Item*

Linking the JIRA work item and the Confluence requirements page is straightforward. Select *Link Issue* and then *Link Confluence* page; see Figure 7-4.

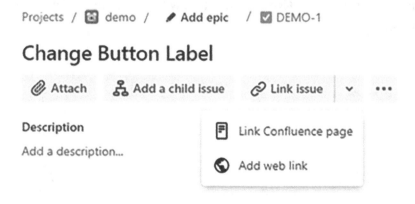

Figure 7-4. *Link JIRA Item*

After you select the *Link Confluence* page, it displays the Confluence Pages search box. Place your cursor and start typing the page name to search for and prepopulate it with the Confluence page. Once you click it, the text box will be filled with URLs. Select the **Link** button, which will complete the linking. See Figure 7-5.

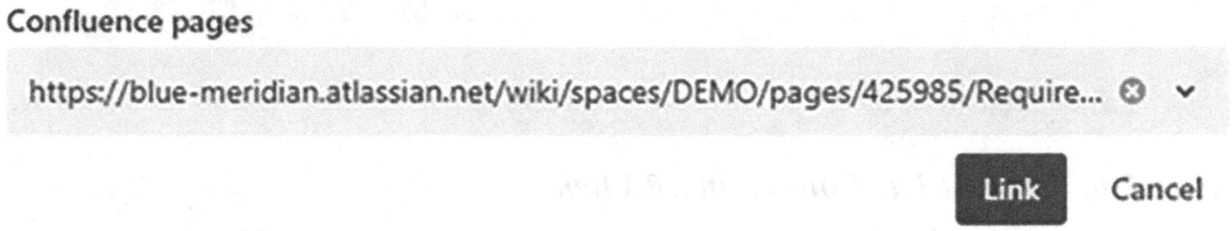

Confluence pages

https://blue-meridian.atlassian.net/wiki/spaces/DEMO/pages/425985/Require... ⊗ ⌄

Link   Cancel

Figure 7-5. *Select Confluence Page to Link*

We will use simple integration between GitLab and JIRA to commit code changes, then mention a JIRA issue ID and see the commit message inside the JIRA issue board. For demonstration purposes, we made a very simple edit—we changed the value for the <title> tag inside the *index.html* page from demo-ui to demo-web using the preferred IDE. Then we commit and push the code changes into the GitLab while adding the DEMO-1 JIRA item ID inside the commit message. See Listing 7-1.

Listing 7-1. Git Commit with JIRA Item ID

```
$git commit -m "Changing label title DEMO-1"

[master dfe34e9] Changing label title DEMO-1
 4 files changed, 53 insertions(+), 1 deletion(-)
...
 create mode 100644 nginx.conf
$git push
...
bbb973c..dfe34e9 master -> master
```

Then we navigate to JIRA and can see the commit message reflected in the item panel. See Figure 7-6.

Taras Gleb 9 minutes ago

Taras Gleb mentioned this issue in a commit of Java Cloud Migration Group / demo-web on branch master:

> Changing label title ☑ DEMO-1: Change Button Label **IN PROGRESS**

Edit · Delete · ☺

Figure 7-6. *View GitLab Commit in JIRA Item*

This type of automation allows the team members to collaborate on the code without interruption and without using additional communication channels, e.g. email.

Output and Deliverables

This section lists deliverables that support software delivery migration. We indicate which deliverable is implemented as part of this book, and which ones are more suitable for enterprise-grade production implementation. In addition, we arbitrarily assign each deliverable to the Product or Platform team, as each IT environment is very distinct and lines of responsibilities could be drawn differently. See Table 7-1.

Table 7-1. *Outputs and Deliverables*

Deliverable	Mandatory	Completed	Team
Sample DevSecOps Flow	Yes	Yes	Product team
GitLab Account	Yes	Yes	Platform/Product team
GitLab Application Code Repository	Yes	Yes	Product team
GitLab Database Code Repository	Yes	Yes	Product team
GitLab Docker Container Repository	Yes	Yes	Product team
GitLab Code Artifactory	Yes	Yes	Product team
GitLab HashiCorp Vault	Yes	Yes	Product team

(continued)

Table 7-1. (*continued*)

Deliverable	Mandatory	Completed	Team
GitLab Checklist to support Definition-of-Done	Yes	Real life	Product team
JIRA Team Account	Yes	Yes	Product team
JIRA Project	Yes	Yes	Product team
JIRA-to-GitLab Integration	Yes	Yes	Platform team
Confluence Team Account	Yes	Yes	Product team
Confluence Project Space	Yes	Yes	Product team
JIRA-to-Confluence Integration	Yes	Yes	Platform team
Tools and processes for performing security and vulnerability scan	Yes	Real life	Product, Platform, and Security teams
Patch management policy for security vulnerabilities	Yes	Real life	Product, Platform, and Security teams
Retention policy for Docker images, configurations, or scripts to manage image lifecycle	Yes	Real life	Platform/Product team

Tools, Techniques and Best Practices

This section provides reference materials for cloud-native, cost-efficient software delivery solutions within the DevSecOps technology and services area. The idea behind the list is that these technologies, tools, and techniques are aligned with the *cloud migration design principles* and allow the team to take full advantage of the *cloud deployment model, the cloud services model, the migration strategies, and the cloud computing characteristics*.

The ultimate objective for the software delivery solution is to help the Product and Platform teams achieve synergy between process, people, and technology organizational factors. This synergy will inevitably allow teams to achieve high-productivity, reduce costs, and deliver high-quality software products. Tools that support agile delivery process, control, and measure work progress, enable collaboration and learning organization with built-in checklists and automated feedback should be part of IT team

DevSecOps toolset. Significant cloud-related cultural change for the IT teams is to realize that software release processes must be fully automated to support agile software delivery to deploy application, infrastructure, and security as a code into an on-premise, public, or hybrid cloud.

Given the high priority of security in the cloud environment, many of these tools introduce various types of security tests for application, containers, and infrastructure code. See Table 7-2.

Table 7-2. *Tools, Techniques, and Best Practices*

Tool, Technique, or Best Practice	Description, Benefits, and Link
Aqua Security	Aqua Security cloud-native comprehensive security solution
Azure DevOps	Azure DevOps Tools
AWS Developer Tools: CodeStar, CodeComit, CodeArtifact, CodeBuild, CodeDeploy, CodePipeline, Cloud9, CloudShell, X-Ray, AWS FIS	AWS Services Developer Tools
Behavior Driven Development (BDD)	Agile software development technique where unit tests are focused on business behavior
Chaos engineering	A testing methodology where team conducts deliberate experimentation and breaks system to understand system's capability to withstand failure
Dependency Check	A software composition analysis tool to detect publicly known vulnerabilities within a project's dependencies
DataOps	Agile methodology for developing and delivering business intelligence and analytics solutions and support data-driven enterprise
Fortify	Automated application security testing tool
FindBugs	An open-source static code analyzer

(continued)

Table 7-2. (*continued*)

Tool, Technique, or Best Practice	Description, Benefits, and Link
GAUNTLT	Provides hooks into security tools to integrate software with various security tests
IAST	An interactive application security testing
IntelliJ Team City	A CICD tool from IntelliJ
OWASP ZAP	OWAST ZAP is an open-source security too for web applications
Nessus Vulnerability Scanner	A remote scanning tool to discover security vulnerabilities
Qualys	Vulnerability management and security solution
ThreadFix	A tool for vulnerability management to organize test results and risk decisions
Test Driven Development (TDD)	Software development technique where software requirements are being converted into test cases before developing software
TestRail	Enterprise test case management software
SAFe	A set of Agile methodology principles and workflow patterns for large enterprises
Scaled Agile Framework (SAFe)	A methodology to implement Agile methodology at the enterprise level
Shift Left Principle	The premise behind this principle is that we move activities typically done at a later stages into earlier phases
SonarQube	A Static Code Analysis tool
Sonartype	Open-source tool to manage risks related to open-source dependency vulnerabilities
WhiteHat	Application security platform

Summary

In this chapter, we continued working on practical understanding of the cloud-native software delivery model. We configured a set of tools that support collaboration and synergy between the core organizational and cloud migration success factors: people, process, and technologies.

These tools are well suited for cloud computing characteristics, as well as service and delivery models and include Atlassian JIRA, Atlassian Confluence, and GitLab.

In the next chapter, we design and implement a sample automated pipeline to deploy software into the cloud environment.

CHAPTER 8

Build Automated Pipeline

Continuous improvement is better than delayed perfection.

— Mark Twain

The idea of automated software delivery has been for the longest time, the proverbial "pot of gold at the end of the rainbow" for the software development industry. After reading and following the instructions in this chapter, you should be able to accomplish the following objective:

- Design and implement an automated DevSecOps pipeline for application, data, configurations, and security within GitLab to deploy, upgrade, roll back, and delete software releases.

To address the "when" question, this step is performed after the team has provisioned the software delivery environment. See Figure 2-3 in Chapter 2 for reference.

The following roles typically contribute to the activities described in this chapter: Developer, Architect, Network Engineer, Infrastructure Engineer, Operations Engineer, Security Engineer, Quality Analyst, Product Owner, and Agile Master.

The arrival of cloud computing has made the need for automated software delivery pipeline both more attainable and more urgent. Support comes with self-service characteristics implemented via cloud provider's data centers API. Urgency stems from complexity of cloud-native deployment models and the need to eliminate manual labor and decrease gaps between infrastructure and application deployments. All this is happening while teams are reducing human error during production deployments and improving software quality, compliance, and security.

Having an automated software pipeline for continuous integration, deployment, and delivery bodes well with the lean production model, fits into the *everything as a service* paradigm, and is a foundation for sustainable competitive advantage and client value delivery. In simple terms, we can deliver customer features to the market faster, without

161

compromising quality, compliance, or security. The development team can benefit from innovations, focus on value-added activities, and automate mundane deployment tasks while freeing time for creative work.

In Chapter 5, we manually deployed application components, packaged inside Docker containers, into the AWS EKS cluster. In this chapter, we design and implement a software delivery pipeline that uses Kubernetes template files from Chapter 5, and we run this pipeline within a software delivery environment (GitLab), provisioned in Chapter 7. This pipeline provides the Product team with continuous integration, continuous deployment and continuous delivery capabilities to deploy, upgrade, roll back, and delete application releases for Dev, QA, UAT, and Prod environments.

Automation pipeline is implemented within the comprehensive DevSecOps platform - GitLab. A real-life GitOps method based scenario would cover infrastructure and application; a pipeline would first provision the required infrastructure, such as a Kubernetes cluster or managed data service, and then build, deploy and test application component and promote data changes. The sample pipeline build presents a simplified use case, where the infrastructure has already been provisioned, and we only design and implement pipeline steps that cover the promotion of the application's backend components.

We have already established units of deployment for our application components; these are Docker containers. The container-build process is somewhat simplified for brevity, e.g. we take the base image from the public DockerHub container repository and reuse it as-is, while adding application code to the base image. Real-life scenarios would involve the Security team responsible for building a base image for the Product team to verify the identity of an image provider, remove unnecessary packages to reduce the surface attack, and apply CIS hardening policies. Positive side effects of compacted image size are faster start-up times as well as reduced storage and networking container related costs. These recommended activities are added to the "Tools, Techniques, and Best Practices" section of the chapter.

In the spirit of following Principle V of The 12-Factor App, we strictly separate the build, release, and run stages in our pipeline implementation: "A codebase is transformed into a (non-development) deploy through three stages:

- The *build* stage converts a code repo into an executable bundle known as a *build*. Using a version of the code at a commit specified by the deployment process, the build stage fetches vendors' dependencies and compiles binaries and assets.

- The *release* stage takes the build produced by the build stage and combines it with deploy's current config. The resulting release contains both the build and the config and is ready for immediate execution in the execution environment.

- The *run* stage (also known as "runtime") runs the app in the execution environment, by launching some set of the app's processes against a selected release."

The CICD mapping to stages, flow, artifacts, and environments is depicted in Figure 8-1.

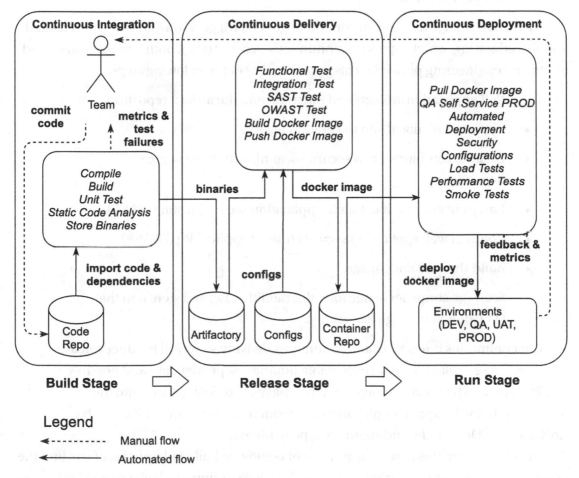

Figure 8-1. The basic CICD pipeline

Pipeline design and implementation starts with the continuous integration (CI) step, which is the process of integrating newly developed code into the existing codebase. Small, frequent changes and merges make it easier and more efficient to isolate and fix any potential issues. During this step, the developer performs the following steps:

- Develop the application feature locally in the IDE of choice.

- Create a pull request.

- Commit the code into the GitLab code repository.

- Build and package application binaries and dependencies.

- Perform unit tests.

Each code change and related commit in general triggers software build and related automated testing, which represents continuous delivery (CD), both a process stage and a software engineering principle. This stage consists of the following steps:

- Pull application artifacts and binaries from the artifact repository.

- Perform functional and integration tests.

- Execute compliance and security scanning for open source dependency.

- Carry out cloud-critical static application security testing (SAST).

- Conduct web application security tests, if applicable (OWASP).

- Build the container image.

- Scan the container image for vulnerabilities, tag and store it in the QA Container Image Repository.

The continuous integration and continuous delivery steps will produce release artifacts. These artifacts contain executable binaries, dependencies, and possibly configurations. The process should sign the images and deploy them into the repository that will support deployment to production environment; it could be Artifactory or Docker, depending on the type of binary.

The last stage in this flow is the process of deploying built and tested artifacts into the production or any other environment, and it's called continuous deployment (CD).

Note   Following the Environment Parity Principle of The 12-Factor App allows for the automated pipeline deployment into the Dev, QA, UAT, and Prod environments with minor variations in the code that describe the cloud environment or deployment steps.

This stage prepares code for operations in the runtime environment. While it may involve additional activities, depending on the team requirements, the following steps satisfy a typical deployment:

- Create or upgrade the AWS EKS cluster (if the GitOps methodology is applied).

- Pull application containers from the QA Docker Container Repository and deploy to the production environment.

- Create database, database schema, and insert data.

- Perform integration, regression, load, smoke, and user acceptance tests.

- Apply policies for network, vulnerability, and compliance security.

After this stage is completed, we have fully deployed application code and configuration, and the latest version of the database running is in the execution environment.

Inputs

To build an automated deployment pipeline, the following inputs are required. This list should be customized to satisfy team requirements and the documentation set.

- GitLab account

- Application code in the GitLab Repository

- Database code in the GitLab Repository

- Application deployment scripts

- Database deployment scripts

- Current application pipeline scripts, configurations, and documentation

- Current application automated tests

- GitLab-to-AWS EKS cluster configuration

- Deployment diagram

- Current state architecture

- Future target state architecture

- Components change summary

- Risk analysis document

- Cloud resources naming and tagging document

- Resource capacity and cost planning document

Process and Activities

The DevSecOps activities conducted in this chapter deliver a sample GitLab automated delivery pipeline. The pipeline code is added to the *.gitlab-ci.yml* file. This file is located in the root directory of *demo-application* project code repository. The GitLab component called Runner uses this file to execute continuous integration, delivery, and deployment jobs defined inside the *.gitlab-ci.yml* file. If you would like to learn more, additional information is available at the following URL: *https://docs.gitlab.com/ee/ development/architecture.html* and *https://docs.gitlab.com/ee/ci/pipelines/*.

The pipeline consists of three stages that compile application code, build the Docker image, store the container image in the internal container repository, and eventually deploy it to the Amazon EKS cluster.

There is a prerequisite to be completed before you can run the pipeline against the AWS EKS cluster. You need to integrate the Amazon Elastic Kubernetes Service (EKS) and the GitLab project. Conveniently, GitLab provides native integration to the AWS Kubernetes cluster.

Prerequisites

We integrate the cluster at the repository project level, but the steps to configure the group or instance level are almost identical.

- *AWS EKS Integration*: To connect a Kubernetes cluster to the project, follow the instructions on the GitLab documentation: Adding and removing Kubernetes clusters.

- *Database connection*: The URL `spring.datasource.url` in the Spring Boot `application.properties` file is pointing to the AWS PostgreSQL RDS service.

GitLab Pipeline

With the connectivity between GitLab and AWS EKS in place, we are now ready to build and execute the GitLab pipeline. We start by adding a pipeline description *.gitlab-ci.yml* YAML file to the root of our project. This file contains step-by-step instructions for the CICD pipeline execution. This could be accomplished in the IDE and then pushed to the code repository or directly in the GitLab. It is one of the convenience features that we will take advantage of. You need *maintainer* or *owner* level access to the project to complete this operation.

Inside GitLab, navigate to project, then choose *Project overview* and *Details*. Choose the branch for the file to be created in, in our case it is `master`. Click the plus icon and choose *New File* with the name set to *.gitlab-ci.yml*. The last step is to commit the changes.

Open and select **Edit** to modify the *.gitlab-ci.yml* file directly in the GitLab interface. Add the contents in Listing 8-1 to the file. The file contains three stages: `build`, `package`, and `deploy`. Each stage will run sequentially and have GitLab jobs added for instruction execution.

Listing 8-1. .gitlab-ci.yml

```
image: docker:latest
services:
  - docker:dind

variables:
  DOCKER_DRIVER: overlay
```

```
stages:
  - build
  - release
  - run

maven-build:
  image: maven:3-jdk-8
  stage: build
  script:
    - echo "Running build:maven-build"
    - mvn package -B
  artifacts:
    paths:
      - target/*.jar

docker-build:
  stage: release
  script:
  - echo "Running package:docker-build"
  - docker build -t registry.gitlab.com/java-cloud-migration-group/demo-
application .
  - docker login -u gitlab-ci-token -p $CI_BUILD_TOKEN registry.gitlab.com
  - docker push registry.gitlab.com/java-cloud-migration-group/demo-
application

deploy:
  stage: run
  image:
    name: bitnami/kubectl:1.14
    entrypoint: [""]
  script:
    - echo "Running deploy:deploy"
    - kubectl delete pod,svc --all --namespace=demo
    - kubectl create -f Deployment.yaml --namespace=demo
    - kubectl create -f Service.yaml   --namespace=demo
    - kubectl get all --namespace=demo
```

```
environment:
  name: dev
  kubernetes:
    namespace: demo
```

Next, click **Commit** to commit the file content to the repository and trigger the pipeline actions. To observe the pipeline execution, click the *CI/CD option* in the GitLab menu on the left. If all jobs execute successfully, there is a green checkmark for each stage/job on the page, as depicted in Figure 8-2.

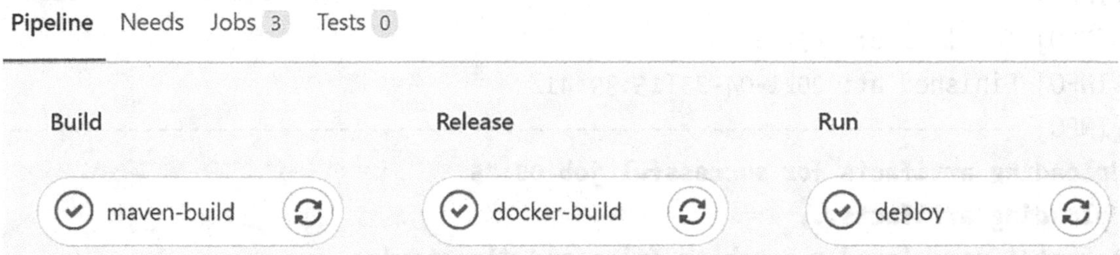

Figure 8-2. *The GitLab pipeline*

Pipeline instructions begin with the **maven-build** job in the build stage, which will build an application *demo-application.jar* file using the Docker container with *maven*. Abbreviated command output for the maven-build job is displayed in Listing 8-2, with important blocks in bold. The last notable step for this job is to upload *demo-application.jar* to the GitLab artifact repository.

Listing 8-2. GitLab Console Abbreviated Maven Build Job Output

Running with gitlab-runner 13.11.0-rc1 (286f7013)
  on docker-auto-scale z3WU8uu-
  feature flags: FF_GITLAB_REGISTRY_HELPER_IMAGE:true
...
Pulling docker image maven:3-jdk-8 ...
Using docker image sha256:8...b45 for maven:3-jdk-8 with digest maven@
sha256:f1..057 ...
Preparing environment 00:01
Running on runner-z3wu8uu--project-24048336-concurrent-0 via runner-
z3wu8uu--srm-1619365012-4ae3d98a...

```
...
$ echo "Running build:maven-build"
Running build:maven-build
$ mvn package -B
[INFO] Scanning for projects...
...
[INFO] Replacing main artifact with repackaged archive
[INFO] ------------------------------------------------------------------
[INFO] BUILD SUCCESS
[INFO] ------------------------------------------------------------------
[INFO] Total time:  45.162 s
[INFO] Finished at: 2021-04-25T15:39:41Z
[INFO] ------------------------------------------------------------------
Uploading artifacts for successful job 00:05
Uploading artifacts...
target/*.jar: found 1 matching files and directories
Uploading artifacts as "archive" to coordinator... ok  id=1210097296
responseStatus=201 Created token=dR-ZCQhY
Cleaning up file based variables 00:00
Job succeeded
```

The following *docker-build* job, which belongs to the package stage, will build the Docker container and tag and push the image to the built-in GitLab Container Repository. See Listing 8-3.

Listing 8-3. GitLab Console Abbreviated Docker Build Job Output

```
Running with gitlab-runner 13.11.0-rc1 (286f7013)
  on docker-auto-scale 0277ea0f
Pulling docker image docker:dind ...
...
...
Downloading artifacts 00:02
Downloading artifacts for maven-build (1210097296)...
Downloading artifacts from coordinator... ok        id=1210097296
responseStatus=200 OK token=dR-ZCQhY
...
```

```
$ echo "Running package:docker-build"
Running package:docker-build
$ docker build -t registry.gitlab.com/java-cloud-migration-group/demo-
application .
Step 1/4 : FROM openjdk:8-jdk-alpine
...
...
Step 4/4 : ENTRYPOINT ["java","-jar","/app.jar"]
...
Successfully built 291233f048fb
Successfully tagged registry.gitlab.com/java-cloud-migration-group/demo-
application:latest
$ docker login -u gitlab-ci-token -p $CI_BUILD_TOKEN registry.gitlab.com
...
Login Succeeded
$ docker push registry.gitlab.com/java-cloud-migration-group/demo-
application
Using default tag: latest
The push refers to repository [registry.gitlab.com/java-cloud-migration-
group/demo-application]
Job succeeded
```

The last step, *deploy* job, which is executed during the deploy stage, will pull the containers from GitLab Container Repository and deploy the image into the AWS EKS cluster that we configured in Chapter 4. The abbreviated output is shown in Listing 8-4, with significant blocks in bold. We execute the kubectl create command to individually to create Deployment and Service Kubernetes objects in the cluster's demo namespace.

Listing 8-4. Deploy Job Output

```
Running with gitlab-runner 13.11.0-rc1 (286f7013)
on docker-auto-scale 72989761
feature flags: FF_GITLAB_REGISTRY_HELPER_IMAGE:true
Preparing the "docker+machine" executor 00:58
Using Docker executor with image bitnami/kubectl:1.14
...
```

```
...
$ echo "Running deploy:deploy"
Running deploy:deploy
$ kubectl delete pod,svc --all --namespace=demo
No resources found
$ kubectl create -f Deployment.yaml --namespace=demo
deployment.apps/demo-service-deployment created
$ kubectl create -f Service.yaml --namespace=demo
service/demo-service-service created
$ kubectl get all --namespace=demo
NAME READY STATUS RESTARTS AGE
pod/demo-service-deployment-667bc47f65-7g4rp 0/1 Pending 0 2s
pod/demo-service-deployment-667bc47f65-wwdsp 0/1 Pending 0 2s
NAME TYPE CLUSTER-IP EXTERNAL-IP PORT(S) AGE
service/demo-service-service
ClusterIP 10.100.168.234 <none> 8080/TCP 1s
NAME READY UP-TO-DATE AVAILABLE AGE
deployment.apps/demo-service-deployment 0/2 2 0 2s
NAME DESIRED CURRENT READY AGE
replicaset.apps/demo-service-deployment-667bc47f65 2 2 0 2s
Cleaning up file based variables 00:00
Job succeeded
```

To verify application deployment, connect to the Amazon EKS cluster using **kubectl**, switch to the AWS EKS context by running the **kubectl config use-context** command, and then validate the installation by running the **kubectl get all -n demo** command; see Listing 8-5.

Listing 8-5. Verify AWS EKS Demo Application Deployment

```
$kubectl config use-context arn:aws:eks:us-east-2:785530736506:cluster/
demo-aws-eks-cluster
Command output
arn:aws:eks:us-east-2:785530736506:cluster/demo-aws-eks-cluster
$kubectl get all -n demo
Command output
```

```
NAME                                            READY    STATUS
    RESTARTS    AGE
pod/demo-service-deployment-667bc47f65-7g4rp    0/1      Pending
    0           1m48s
pod/demo-service-deployment-667bc47f65-wwdsp    0/1      Pending
    0           1m48s

NAME                            TYPE       CLUSTER-IP     EXTERNAL-IP
    PORT(S)      AGE
service/demo-service-service    ClusterIP  10.100.168.234
    <none>          8080/TCP    8m47s

NAME                                       READY    UP-TO-DATE
    AVAILABLE    AGE
deployment.apps/demo-service-deployment    0/2      2
0           8m49s

NAME                                            DESIRED
    CURRENT    READY    AGE
replicaset.apps/demo-service-deployment-667bc47f65    2
2           0        8m49s

C:\Users\tgleb>
```

Our deployment job is utilizing individual **kubectl** commands for each template file, which could be somewhat suitable for development, but inefficient to deploy real-life applications into production environments. One of the recommended practices is to apply the Helm *(https://helm.sh/)* Kubernetes package manager. You will find information about recommended best practices in the "Tools, Techniques, and Best Practices" section later in this chapter.

Output and Deliverables

Deliverables in this chapter focus on pipeline implementation for automated CI/CD process, and the list for this step in cloud migration is quite extensive. Each deliverable includes a note to indicate whether it was implemented here, or is recommended for an enterprise-grade production implementation by either the Product or Platform team. See the list of deliverables in Table 8-1.

Table 8-1. *Outputs and Deliverables*

Deliverable	Mandatory	Completed	Team
GitLab CICD pipeline implementation	Yes	Yes	Product or Platform team
Docker images are deployed to the Kubernetes cluster	Yes	Yes	Product or Platform team
Resource naming policies, e.g. Azure Naming Convention in GitHub	Yes	No	Product or Platform team
RBAC security policies are defined, including RBAC roles	Yes	No	Product, or Platform, (Security) teams
Appropriate Git Flow Model (selected prior to pipeline implementation)	Yes	No	Product or Platform team
Base secure Docker container image selected for application and any dependency, either open-source based image or vendor	Yes	No	Product or Platform team (Infrastructure, Security)
GitLab CICD Pipeline Workflow Diagram	Yes	No	Product team
Application dependencies built as part of the pipeline	Yes	Yes	Product or Platform team
Unit, functional, regression, security, performance, sanity and smoke tests; determined when to run in pipeline; including provisioning any dependency, such as integration, database, etc.	Yes	No	Product team
Quality Assurance tests included as part of automated pipeline resulting in PASS/FAIL	Yes	No	Product team
Database is created as part of testing: -Database schema is created -Test data is inserted into the database -Automated and repeatable process to create empty database, database roles, and empty schema instance	Yes	No	Product team

(continued)

Table 8-1. (*continued*)

Deliverable	Mandatory	Completed	Team
Retention policy for docker images and clean-up automation	Yes	No	Product team
Application components built as containers with Helm packages	Yes	No	Product team
Docker images are tagged and stored in the Container Repository	Yes	No	Product team
Monitoring, logging, and alerting is configured and deployed as part of the automated pipeline	Yes	No	Product or Platform team
Application configurations and feature management are applied	Yes	No	Product team
Chaos engineering testing designed and implemented as part of the pipeline	Yes	No	Product Team
Application code security and vulnerability tests as part of the pipeline e.g. SAST, DAST, OWASP	Yes	No	Product or Platform (Security) team
Dependency checking as part of the pipeline for security vulnerabilities	Yes	No	Product or Platform (Security) team
Documentation, test results, and release notes, dependency checking, and any verifications reports published as part of build process	Yes	No	Product or Platform (Security) team
Security scanning for Docker containers completed as part of the pipeline	Yes	No	Product or Platform (Security) team
Patch management policies for third-party software vulnerabilities are defined	Yes	No	Product or Platform team (Infrastructure, Security)
Versioning mechanism designed and applied for application, Helm packages, Docker images	Yes	No	Product team

(*continued*)

Table 8-1. (*continued*)

Deliverable	Mandatory	Completed	Team
Configurations for Request and Limits are mandatory and part of the pipeline, resulting in PASS/FAIL outcome for Cost and Resource Management	Yes	No	Product team
Tags and labels are mandatory and specified for cost and resource management, resulting in PASS/FAIL outcome for Cost and Resource Management	Yes	No	Product team
DORA metrics—Deployment Frequency (DF), Mean Lead Time for changes (MLT), Mean Time to Recover (MTTR) and Change Failure Rate (CFR)—to evaluate migration progress velocity and quality for Project Management	Yes	No	Product team
Base Docker image: signature verification	Yes	No	Product or Platform team
Base Docker image: remove unneeded packages	Yes	No	Product or Platform team
Base Docker image: apply required packages as needed	Yes	No	Product or Platform team
Base Docker image: apply hardening policies as per CIS	Yes	No	Product or Platform team
Base Docker image: create new Image	Yes	No	Product or Platform team
Base Docker image: make image single-layered	Yes	No	Product or Platform team
Base Docker image: sign image	Yes	No	Product or Platform team
Base Docker image: store in common repository	Yes	No	Product or Platform team
Passwords and Secrets are stored in Vault Repository	Yes	No	Product or Platform team

Tools, Techniques and Best Practices

This section provides reference materials for cloud-native, cost-efficient software delivery solutions (in the DevSecOps technology and services area). The idea behind the list is that these technologies, tools, and techniques are aligned with the *cloud migration design principles* and allow the team to take full advantage of the *cloud deployment model, the cloud services model, the migration strategies, and the cloud computing characteristics.*

The ultimate objective is to provide readers with a good starting point that helps design, implement, and operate cloud-native, reliable, high-quality, and secure software delivery automation solution. The solution proposed here is cloud-provider and vendor-agnostic and substantially reduces or completely eliminates non-value added manual tasks. Team will benefit from innovations provided by the comprehensive DevSecOps platform.

Key point to keep in mind is that, when implementing the software delivery automation, the solution should be comprehensive and inclusive. In addition to classic compile, test, build, and package steps, we must incorporate a suite of functions for quality, reliability, cost-efficiency, security, and compliance that encompasses the entire stack: infrastructure and application.

Given that public cloud providers are using commodity computing in their data centers, *chaos engineering* has emerged as a risk mitigation strategy to defend against possible future failures in infrastructure and networking, and guarantee application resiliency in the distributed computing environment. The list of suggested best tools, techniques, and best practices is presented in Table 8-2.

Table 8-2. *Tools, Techniques, and Best Practices*

Tool, Technique, or Best Practice	Description/Benefits
Architecture Fitness Functions: Performance, Cost Efficiency	A function (similar to unit test) that tests particular non-functional characteristic of the software solution
Azure Naming Convention on GitHub	Labeling for cost management Labeling for network and operational security

(continued)

Table 8-2. (*continued*)

Tool, Technique, or Best Practice	Description/Benefits
Chef and Puppet	A suite of software tool to enable Continuous Delivery capability
Configuration as a Service	Configuration approach where application configurations are obtained from a service and not from the runtime environment
Dynamic Application Security Testing (DAST)	Approach to security testing where vulnerabilities or weaknesses are found in a running application; also known as "black box" testing
D2IQ	A CICD software vendor that provides a set of tools for automated management of Kubernetes
Feature Management as a Service	SaaS to manage and control features flags that helps ease complexities managing feature delivery to the customers
Helm	*A* Kubernetes package manage
Interactive Application Security Testing (IAST)	Approach to security testing that was created to address shortcomings of SAST and DAST; it tests data flows inside the application
Kubernetes Resource Request and Limits	Resource request and limits configuration restrict how much compute resources a given pod can request
Mobile Application Security Testing (MAST)	Approach to security testing that includes authentication, authorization, data, and session security within mobile applications
Runtime Application Self Protection (RASP)	Security methodology that runs continuous security check on the application in the environment and responds to the attach by terminating attacker's session
Red Hat Ansible	A software deliver automation platform
Static Application Security Testing (SAST)	Approach to secure software by reviewing the source code or "white box" testing

Summary

Deliverables in this chapter covered the implementation aspect of the DevSecOps services and technology area and are represented by a GitLab pipeline for automated continuous integration, continuous delivery, and continuous deployment. Developers benefit from one of the key cloud computing characteristics: on-demand self-service and provisioning of resources.

Having automated code that builds, tests, and deploys full application stack, provides repeatability and correctness the first time and every time. It goes further to include automated upgrade, rollback, and delete operations. In essence, the automated pipeline provides high-velocity, agile software delivery without compromising quality, security, or compliance. Introduction of GitOps and Kubernetes along with the declarative over imperative deployment approach bring a high degree of automation in context of system administration, where software as opposed to humans monitors the system and brings it to the desired state.

The self-provisioning aspect of cloud computing, supported by automated pipelines, greatly reduces non-value adding activities, introduces incremental innovations, and allows teams to focus on writing business code or enhance automation. Shifting testing and security to the left stops bugs or security breaches before they can reach production. We were able to achieve a high degree of cloud maturity via GitLab SaaS utilization.

After the application has been deployed, we are ready to look into effective cloud operations. In the next chapters, we will answer the following questions: what entails efficient cloud-native resources and cost management, how do we successfully finalize migration from on-premises to the cloud, and where will our disaster recovery environment be implemented?

PART IV

Software Operations Migration

Part IV provides a deep-dive into the software operations (Ops) technology and service area, as depicted in Figure IV-1.

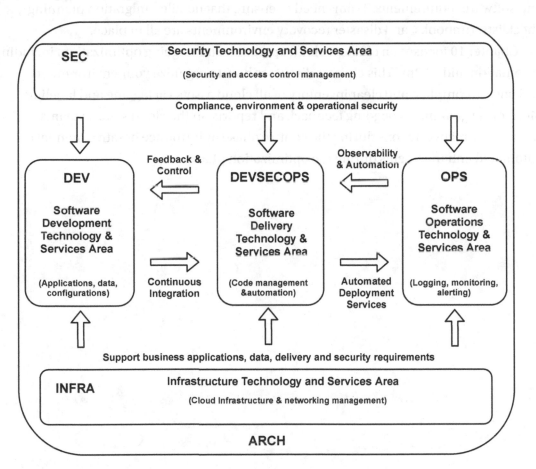

Figure IV-1. *Cloud migration technology and services areas*

The main focus is on the final steps in cloud adoption: software operations migration. They are critical for business value realization through continuing and cost-efficient operation of technology assets deployed to the cloud. Executed properly, they take full advantage of core cloud computing characteristics, including self-provisioning, metered compute resources and automated elasticity to ensure a lean production environment, where workload requirements are closely matched to the provisioned resources and fluctuate in sync. Unfortunately, the opposite is also true. Steps implemented incorrectly cause cloud cost overruns and increased maintenance effort and ultimately could worsen a firm's competitive position.

Chapter 9 presents a complete software operations migration process, which consists of the following: preparing, planning, migrating, controlling, and optimizing. It starts with a detailed planning step, which uses inputs from previous chapters. One such example is a deployment diagram, which helps the teams understand hardware and software requirements. Teams need to ensure that detailed migration planning checklists, runbooks, and disaster recovery environments are all in place.

Chapter 10 focuses on efficient cloud operation and ongoing optimization, including automation and AIOps. This chapter discusses how to organize your environments and ensure complete and clear inventory of all cloud assets via tagging and labeling. Monitoring guarantees ongoing feedback and reports on the cloud state so teams can take corrective actions during the control phase or introduce iterative manual or automated enhancements during the optimization phase.

CHAPTER 9

Transition, Runbook and Disaster Recovery

If you fail to plan, you are planning to fail!

— Benjamin Franklin

This chapter is the last mile before the migration finish line. On one hand it is one of the riskiest in terms of scope, importance, and impact, yet it is also the most rewarding in terms of accomplishment. It focuses on promoting application, data, and services into the Production cloud environments and servicing client requests from that environment, as opposed to the datacenter.

After reading and following the instructions in this chapter, you should be able to accomplish the following objectives:

- Develop a detailed *migration readiness checklist* and *production migration plan* to capture mandatory activities (including rollback) and resolve the impact within an enterprise and across external stakeholders.

- Develop a *cloud operations runbook* to ensure smooth and express resolution of any post-migration or operational incidents.

- Design, document, implement, and test a *disaster recovery (DR)* solution.

To address the "when" question, this migration step is performed when the team deploys application and data to the cloud provider infrastructure production environment and starts servicing client requests exclusively from this environment. See Figure 2-3 in Chapter 2 for reference.

© Taras Gleb 2021
T. Gleb, *Systematic Cloud Migration*, https://doi.org/10.1007/978-1-4842-7252-7_9

The following roles typically contribute to the activities described in this chapter: Developer, Architect, Operations Engineer, Quality Analyst, Product Owner, Agile Master, Operations, Legal, Client Services, and Sales and other departments, including external stakeholders.

To ensure technology (architecture, development, infrastructure) and documentation deliverables are accurately completed and accounted for, we start with the application migration readiness checklist. We conduct impact analysis across three major areas: *IT teams, the company's internal department, and the external stakeholders.* See Figure 9-1.

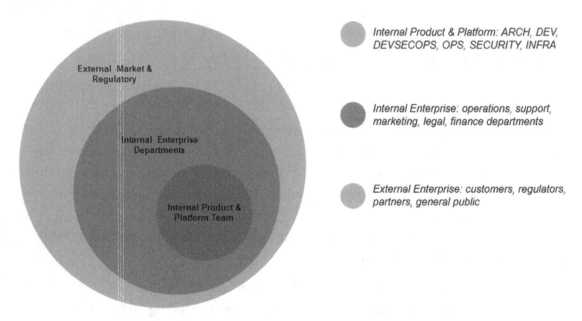

Figure 9-1. *Migration impact analysis and planning areas*

The objective is to identify gaps in deliverables within and particularly across each boundary. This analysis is typically conducted inside out. We start with the narrowest scope, the Product and Platform teams. Team analysis is focused on deliverables in all major services and technology areas: Arch, Dev, DevSecOps, Ops, Security, and Infra. The subsequent scope is concerned with impact analysis across different departments within the organization. Examples of dependencies includes Customer Support, Operations, Legal, Compliance, Finance, and Account Management. We need to take into consideration that migration information needs to be communicated and ensure that the appropriate actions are taken in these departments. Additionally, these departments might need to notify external customers, clients, regulators, or the general public. This flow of information, departments, and processes may add further lead time to associated deliverables. Information elicited during this exercise is collected in the *production migration plan*, which becomes the central place for migration communication, coordination, planning, execution, and control.

To protect production environments and data from failure and give confidence to business and IT management, we need to design, document, implement, and test the *disaster recovery* solutions. There are various ways to implement the solution in the cloud; from IaaS-based in-house implementation to Disaster Recovery as a Service (DRaaS) by the third-party providers. DR requirements, the simplest of which are Recovery Time Objectives (RTO), Recovery Point Objectives (RPO), and Service Level Agreement (SLA) metrics, are provided as input to the DR design documents and subsequent implementation, to ensure they are met before migration is completed.

Another deliverable is the *cloud operations runbook*. We use the term *runbook* going forward in this text for brevity. It supports seamless transition and provides resolution steps after migration or operational incidents or Day 2. Examples of the information included in the runbook are the login URL for the Kibana or Grafana dashboards, contact information for escalation and incident resolutions, how to stop or start the system, etc.

To conduct the cutover to the cloud, the teams typically set up a war room on the day of the migration, with all the needed resources at the table to help resolve issues as they arise. The collective of the artifacts and deliverables described here provides a go/no-go decision point during the migration process.

Inputs

The following base set of inputs are required for migration planning and execution:

- Future target state architecture
- Components change summary
- Risk analysis document
- Resource capacity and cost planning

It is expected that you will add more inputs, given your specific migration scenarios and requirements.

Processes and Activities

We start with creating a *migration readiness checklist,* which covers all technology and service areas. The idea is similar to the list that NASA goes through every time a rocket is launched into space.

Each area in the checklist has clearly defined activities and objectives, against which we verify readiness. Next, we move on to building a *production migration plan,* which represents a detailed and comprehensive D-day flow for switchover to the cloud production environment. Before we move the production code into the cloud provider environment, we design, document, and test the disaster recovery solutions.

The last activity is to implement the *cloud operations runbook* to provide full visibility and establish clearly defined ownership of the application, the data, and the services in the cloud.

Migration Readiness Checklist

At this point, there should not be any missing software artifacts or documentation to complete the migration process. We will take the full inventory of the deliverables from the previous migration steps and collect them into the checklist document grouped by technology and services areas. The objective is to ensure that deliverables are completed and activities and artifacts are aligned with the overall migration goal and that they benefit from cloud computing characteristics:

- *Development (Dev):* Application components, data, and services are refactored for cloud migration; all environments are provisioned, including automated pipelines that supports full development lifecycle and portability, reliability, and resiliency.

- *Architecture (Arch)*: Migration is clearly understood, documented, and communicated; critical decisions are captured, reviewed, and agreed upon.

- *Infrastructure (Infra):*

  - Cloud provider resources are provisioned, organized, tagged, and documented. Automation provisioning scripts are checked into the code repository.

  - The DR solution is designed, documented, and tested with failover automation.

- *DevSecOps (DevSecOps):* Infrastructure, application, data, and configurations are deployable via an automated pipeline with quality checkpoints in place to satisfy observability, quality, automation, and reliability requirements.

- *Security (Sec):* Security processes, checks, and configurations are completed and implemented as part of the automated pipeline.

- *Operations (Ops):*

  - Processes that address automation, reporting, visibility, ownership, and supportability are in place. All cloud operational processes are documented (e.g., the runbook), access to all environments is granted as required per security RBAC and ACL lists.

  - A full stack monitoring, logging, and alerting solution is designed, documented, and implemented to support observability, quality, reliability, and automation.

Each area's tasks and deliverables are summarized in Table 9-1.

Table 9-1. *Migration Readiness Checklist*

Area	Process and Activities	Deliverable
Arch	Perform application analysis, plan, and document migration strategy and cloud provider selection Document and communicate future target architecture to describe desired system state for cloud migration	• Solution architecture document • Current state architecture • Future state architecture • System context diagram • Components diagram • Deployment diagram • Risk analysis document
Infra	Build robust, secure, and cost-efficient cloud environment for application components and database, which consist of IAM services, AWS EKS cluster, PostgreSQL SaaS, networking, and storage	• Cloud resources naming and tagging • AWS EKS Cluster • AWS PostgreSQL RDS • Resource Capacity and cost planning document • Disaster recovery environment
Dev	Migrate application data to AWS PostgreSQL RDS Migrate configurations into ConfigMap and deploy to the Kubernetes cluster Package components into Docker containers and push images to DockerHub Generate Kubernetes YAML templates files for deployments and services Manually deploy application components with template files in the Kubernetes cluster	• Component change summary • Application code in the Git Repository • Database code in the Git Repository • Docker containers in the GitHub Container Repository • Applications logging configurations • Applications monitoring configurations • Applications alerting configurations • Application security configurations • Applications runtime configurations • Database security configurations • Application delivery process • Database delivery process • Application deployment scripts • Database deployment scripts • Definition of done checklist

(continued)

Table 9-1. (*continued*)

Area	Process and Activities	Deliverable

DevSecOps	Configure tools for cloud-native software delivery environments: JIRA, Confluence, and GitLab
	
	Design and implement automated DevSecOp pipeline for application, data, configurations, and security within GitLab to deploy, upgrade, roll back, and delete software releases
		• Software delivery environments
		  • JIRA
		  • Confluence
		  • GitLab
		• Automated delivery pipeline in GitLab

Security	Secure cluster, database service, network, and storage Complete security processes and checks as part of the automated pipeline	• Security migration readiness checklist • Security pipeline steps • Data flow diagram for security, legal, and compliance

Ops	Plan, organize, monitor, control, and optimize cloud technology assets utilization
	
	Establish efficient cost management, plan workload resources, create and maintain assets inventory, monitor and control utilization rate, and apply manual and/ or automated (policy-based or machine learning-based) optimization practices
	
	Develop a cost-conscious organization
		• Cloud operations runbook
		• Monitoring, logging, and alerting implementation
		  • Prometheus, Grafana
		  • Elasticsearch, FluentBit, Kibana
		  • PagerDuty
		• Monitoring, logging, and alerting handbook
		• Application migration readiness checklist
		• Production migration plan
		• Disaster recovery document
		• Cost management document

At this moment we have prepared a full inventory of cloud migration deliverables and can move ahead to design and implement the production migration plan.

Production Migration Plan

In the same way that the migration readiness checklist builds on an existing set of deliverables, the production migration plan is assembled around software delivery flow. The idea is to reuse and organize processes for smooth transitions from existing production environments to the cloud provider infrastructure. Granted, it may not be an easy task, as in some scenarios, existing production environments have substantial amounts of legacy technologies and integrations, sometimes to the external organizations and way outside of the control of the current Product or Platform teams. Another set of constraints comes from business, legal, and compliance areas; e.g., we need to obtain customer's consent to move their data to the public cloud provider's infrastructure or release this information into the public domain that might affect the company's stock price and stakeholders' value.

The production migration plan designed here will consist of four high-level stages:

- *Prepare:*

    - Identify and provide prerequisites and resolution steps infernally within enterprise and across external stakeholders—customers, regulators, vendors, and partners.

    - Communicate and coordinate resolution and planning steps across internal and external stakeholders.

- *Plan*: Detailed migration process that takes into consideration all prerequisites from the preparation stage. Migration process should consist of unambiguous and concrete actions (commands) that are idempotent and reversible.

- *Execute*: Execute migration plans by Product and Platform teams, including pre- and post-deployment steps. Typically this stage reuses software artifacts, environments, and automated pipelines developed in previous steps, including rollback capabilities.

- *Control*: Provide control and post-migration operations and communication to all stakeholders.

This flow is captured in Figure 9-2 and reflects both high-level stages and detailed steps to complete the cutover to the cloud provider production environment. In a typical scenario, this plan would be implemented using the war-room approach, where all the technical and non-technical resources are colocated for unrestricted communication and quick resolution for any problem that might arise during migration. Resources not available for colocation should be in the online meeting with screen sharing, and should be a set of go/no-go points in the process.

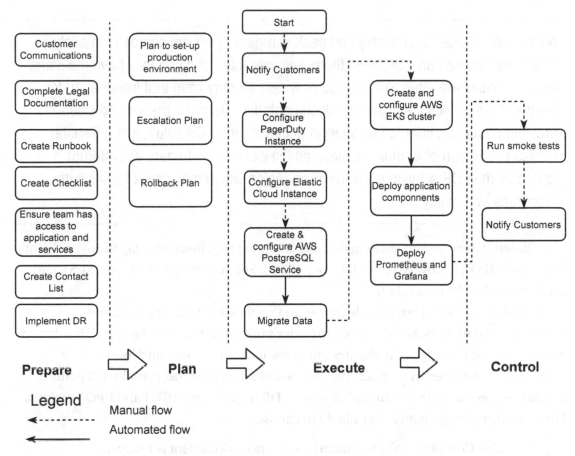

Figure 9-2. Production migration plan

The migration plan presented in this text is a simplified model for demonstration purposes and to clarify the concept. Real-life scenarios are characterized by more complex dependencies, processes, and stakeholders, which must be all taken into consideration to ensure a successful and smooth transition on the day of migration.

Disaster Recovery

Prior to migration, the team designs, implements, and tests DR solutions for the entire technology stack, where automated failover and restore should be in place between primary and backup regions.

Note   When selecting primary and backup regions, perform comparison analysis to ensure service parity between them, because that not all regions have the same set of services available. Some cloud providers already have that information for DR purposes. Check the provider's documentation. Decide if the second cloud provider should be selected as a target deployment for DR solution. If a disaster strikes one region of a single provider, all the existing customers will attempt to deploy their DR solution in the back-up region which may cause issues with resources availability.

DR design begins with eliciting and documenting requirements; e.g. Recovery Point Objective (RPO), Recovery Time Objective (RTO), Service Level Agreement (SLA), and Service Level Objectives (SLO).

The DR solution for our sample four-tiered application includes the client, web, business and data tiers, and the cloud provider's infrastructure. We design a DR solution that utilizes the provider's capabilities and benefits from services and innovations within the disaster recovery space. We review and select the most suitable DR pattern, additionally evaluated with simplified cost vs. DR requirement (RTO and RPO) analysis. There are three major patterns available to choose from:

- *Hot:* Complete, fully resourced duplicate environment is ready to take over for the primary at all times. This is the most expensive and most complex solution to design, but provides the shortest possible, virtually zero, downtime RTO.

- *Warm:* Minimal duplicate system is ready; however, only the bare minimum services are up and running at all times. This approach is the next most expensive, but is faster to return to service than a Cold restoration, with possibly some downtime or interruptions.

- *Cold:* No alternative failover resources are kept running. This requires a complete rebuild of the application and data environment (preferably via automation). Because no failover resources are kept running, this design is the cheapest, but takes the longest to execute and might include downtime and interruption.

This sample application uses the following AWS services: EKS for Web and Business Tiers, AWS IAM, AWS EC2, and AWS PostgreSQL RDS for Data Tier. After conducting rudimentary RTO and RPO vs. cost analysis, we propose the DR solution outlined in Table 9-2.

Table 9-2. *Cloud Disaster Recovery*

Tier	Proposed Solution	Building Block
Web tier	Create an EKS cluster in the failover region, preferably by automation. Deploy application components using DR configured GitLab automated pipeline.	AWS EKS Cluster GitLab
Business tier		
Data tier	Cross-region automated asynchronous replication, to Read Replica, where backups and snapshots are stored in an S3 bucket with tiered pricing applied to the stored data, based on time horizon. In case of failover, the Read Replica is promoted to Master.	AWS PostgreSQL RDS S3
Infrastructure tier	Some of the AWS Services, such as IAM, are global and do not need replication. Others, such as virtual machines and networking gear, could be re-created in the failover region.	AWS EC2, including virtual machines and networking gear

DR flow, similar to the migration plan, consists of specific and unambiguous steps that are idempotent and reversible. Real-life failover flows are software product and individual environment specific and are designed by the Product team. The primary objective is to reach a level of automation where the failover process is partially or fully automated and downtime is minimized. The sample flow is presented in Figure 9-3 and it consists of three distinct phases:

- *Prepare:* This phase is focused on solution design and implementation. The team prepares a GitLab automated pipeline for the application components failover and configures AWS PostgreSQL Service replication and backup options.

- *Automated Failover:* This phase typically is triggered when a DR event has occurred and consists of steps that fail over all application services to the backup region.

- *Test and Cleanup:* This phase is focused on full restoration of services and any required post-deployment or cleanup tasks.

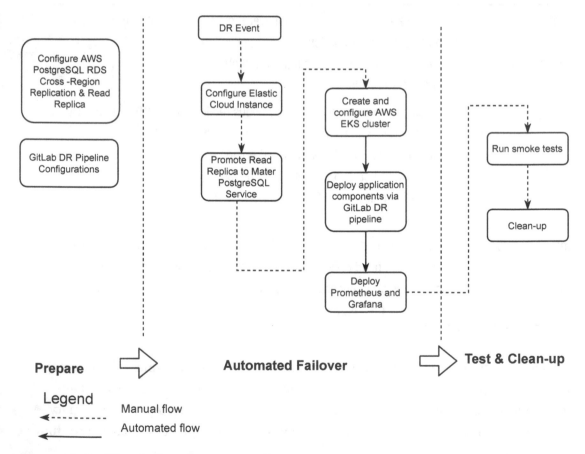

Figure 9-3. *Cloud disaster recovery flow*

Having a robust DR solution prevents costly interruption to the business process and loss of data. It allows for the system to be relocated to the backup location within the RTO and RPO objectives.

Cloud Operations Runbook

To document the cloud environment administration steps and issue the resolution processes and the system's access information, we discuss the *cloud operations runbook*. Information collected in the runbook describes routines such as starting or stopping the system, accessing different components, and debugging and resolving issues in a standard, repeatable, and efficient way. The runbook is part of the Information Technology Infrastructure Library (ITIL), represents the building blocks of knowledge management, and helps build learning organizations for the cloud environments.

It is important for the runbook to be accurate, actionable, and adaptable. Runbooks come in a two flavors—*general* and *specialized*—and can be of three types, depending on the degree of automation:

- *Manual*: All steps are performed by a human operator

- *Semi-automated*: A combination of manual steps and automated tasks

- *Automated:* No human intervention

The runbook details for our sample application, AWS infrastructure, and software delivery migration environment are presented in Table 9-3.

Table 9-3. *The Cloud Migration Runbook*

Category	Description
Environments information	This section includes URLs for production environments for application, data, and any tools and software that are required for normal operations. • AWS Console • AWS PostgreSQL RDS • JIRA • GitLab • Prometheus • Grafana • PagerDuty • Elasticsearch • Kibana
Login information	This section includes login information (user credentials) for all applications and data and any tools and software that are required for normal operations. • AWS Console • AWS PostgreSQL RDS • JIRA • GitLab • Prometheus • Grafana • PagerDuty • Elasticsearch • Kibana

(continued)

Table 9-3. (*continued*)

Category	Description
Configuration information	This section includes configuration information for all applications and data and any tools and software that are required for normal operations. • AWS Console • AWS PostgreSQL RDS • JIRA • GitLab • Prometheus • Grafana • PagerDuty • Elasticsearch • Kibana
Logging, monitoring, alerting, and escalation procedures	This section typically describes the following processes: • How to access and analyze log files inside Kibana • How to access and analyze application metrics in Grafana • What alerts are generated, and how to access alerts and resolve them in PagerDuty • What are the escalation procedure, timelines, and contacts
Operational and maintenance procedures	This section includes details for processes and steps related to regular maintenance tasks, such as: • Start or stop the AWS PostgreSQL service • Back up data in the AWS PostgreSQL service • Start or stop the AWS EKS cluster • Check your worker nodes in the AWS EKS cluster, and scale, drain or delete as required
Production failure and recovery procedures	This section typically details the following processes: • How to resolve issues with application components running in the AWS EKS cluster • How to resolve issues with the AWS PostgreSQL database service

(*continued*)

Table 9-3. (*continued*)

Category	Description
Disaster Recovery procedures	This section typically provides resolution steps for the following content: • What is the DR failover criteria • What are the RTO and RPO objectives • What is the DR process (manual or automated), including pre- and post-migration verification steps • Information about DR environments

Runbooks guarantee reliable, consistent, and high-quality delivery of business applications to the cloud provider's environment. They represent a proactive strategy that allows teams to resolve issues more quickly and in a structured and repeatable manner, as well as share the knowledge and automate recovery steps in the future.

Output and Deliverables

The list of deliverables in this chapter focuses on migration planning into cloud production environments. The list could be extended or adopted to fit particular migration requirements, scenarios, and environments. We started with the application *migration readiness checklist* and the *production migration plan* to capture mandatory migration artifacts and activities. We move on to the *cloud operations runbook* for smooth production transition and documented resolutions for post-migration incidents, and designed a sample disaster recovery plan.

Each deliverable includes a note that indicates whether it was implemented here, or is recommended for an enterprise-grade production implementation by either the Product or Platform team. See the list of deliverables in Table 9-4.

Table 9-4. *Outputs and Deliverables*

Deliverable	Mandatory	Completed	Team
Application migration readiness checklist	Yes	Yes	Product team
Security migration readiness checklist	Yes	No	Platform team
Production migration plan (including rollback)	Yes	Yes	Product and Platform teams
Disaster Recovery (DR) document	Yes	Yes	Product and Platform teams
Cloud operations runbook (including escalation plan, alert destination configuration, on-call personnel identification, on-duty managers, escalation sr. managers)	Yes	No	Product and Platform teams
Cloud production environment	Yes	No	Product or Platform teams
Legal documentation and privacy statements	Yes	No	Legal team
Cloud environment RBAC	Yes	No	Product or Platform teams
Cloud environment ACL	Yes	No	Product or Platform team
Contact information list	Yes	No	Product or Platform team
Customer communication plan	Yes	No	Product or Platform team
Billing and licensing documentation	Yes	No	Product or Platform team
Cloud Disaster Recovery (DR) environment	Yes	No	Product or Platform team
DR database replication implementation	Yes	No	Product or Platform team

(*continued*)

Table 9-4. (*continued*)

Deliverable	Mandatory	Completed	Team
DR application migration scripts or automation implementation	Yes	No	Product or Platform team
Automation or scripts for monitoring, logging, alerting, and DR implementation	Yes	No	Product or Platform team

Tools, Techniques and Best Practices

This section provides reference materials for cloud-native, cost-efficient software delivery solutions within the DevSecOps Technology and Services area. The idea behind the list is that these technologies, tools, and techniques are aligned with the *cloud migration design principles* and allow the team to take full advantage of the *cloud deployment model, the cloud services model, the migration strategies, and the cloud computing characteristics*. See Table 9-5.

Table 9-5. *Tools, Techniques, and Best Practices*

Tool, Technique, or Best Practice	Description/Benefits
AWS Architecture Blog: Disaster Recovery	AWS architecture center blog best practices on DR solutions
AWS Well Architectured Concepts Runbook	Runbook provides documented processes to successfully execute support procedures
Azure Backup and Disaster Recovery	Azure backup and DR guidelines and solutions
DRaaS	Disaster Recovery as a Service is a cloud computing delivery model to back-up infrastructure and data using third-party provider environment and orchestration service
Microsoft Azure Site Recovery	Microsoft Azure DR service
Quorum on DRaaS	Quorum DR service

(*continued*)

Table 9-5. (*continued*)

Tool, Technique, or Best Practice	Description/Benefits
Readiness Checklist	Checklist to prepare environment for migration, including preparing the blueprint and growing it
Google Architecture Center Disaster Recovery	Google Architecture Center set of best practices and recommendations on DR solutions
Zerto Virtual Replication	Zerto DR service

Summary

This chapter covered planning and production environment migration from an on-premise datacenter to a cloud provider infrastructure. It is one of the most challenging step when applications have extensive legacy integrations in regard to technologies or external dependencies.

Deliverables included a *migration readiness checklist, a production migration plan, a disaster recovery (DR) solution,* and a *cloud operations runbook.*

You are ready to move on to the next and final step in this journey. Chapter 10 covers cloud-native operations.

CHAPTER 10

Cloud Native Operations

However beautiful the strategy, you should occasionally look at the results.

— Winston Churchill

Congratulations! If you are reading this chapter and have completed all the previous ones, including the practical exercises, you have crossed the proverbial migration finish line. You provisioned cost-efficient, reliable, secure, and observable operational environments on the cloud provider infrastructure and deployed application code and data via an automated pipeline within the comprehensive DevSecOps ecosystem!

After reading and following the instructions in this chapter, you should be able to accomplish the following objectives:

- Develop a fundamental understanding of the *cloud-native software operational model* and its building blocks.

- Plan, organize, monitor, control, and optimize *cost-efficient cloud software operations*.

To address the "when" question, this step is performed before and after (ongoing) production environment is migrated to the cloud. See Figure 2-3 in Chapter 2 for reference.

The following roles typically contribute to the activities described in this chapter: Developer, Architect, Operations Engineer, Quality Analyst, Product Owner, and Agile Master.

This chapter is focused on the Ops technology and service area and it guides you through Day 2 operations, which is concerned with an application running in the cloud provider's infrastructure after the migration has been completed. Operational IT models within the last decade have been gradually evolving from classic ITOps to *CloudOps*, which is an umbrella term for a set of GitOps, DataOps, MLOps, AIOps and

© Taras Gleb 2021
T. Gleb, *Systematic Cloud Migration*, https://doi.org/10.1007/978-1-4842-7252-7_10

XOps (everything as Ops). The next step in the evolutional maturity process are AIOps recommendations engines, referred to in the "Tools, Techniques, and Best Practices" section later in this chapter. All these models intrinsically take advantage of cloud computing characteristics and delivery and service models. The XOps methodologies are born and built on a paradigm change, which shifts software operations to rapid, elastic, and metered infrastructures that match workloads for cost efficiency. It's aided by automated deployment, with a built-in shared responsibility security model, and all-inclusive observability for the entire hardware and software stack.

Cloud-native operations and related principles of operational excellence are supported by a set of building blocks completed throughout this book. Let's recap and recognize each artifact's contribution to these operational practices before we deep dive into the main subject of this chapter: efficient cost management.

- *Part I: Introduction to Cloud Computing:*

    - Chapter 1 introduced essential cloud computing concepts and built foundational knowledge for the rest of the book.

    - Chapter 2 established organizational capabilities in the core areas of people, processes, and technologies and introduced migration design and implementation blocks in the form of maturity models, migration strategies, design principles, and cloud-native technologies.

- *Part II: Software Development Migration*

    - Chapter 3 developed a cloud-native target architecture state to satisfy performance, scalability, reliability, and testability of non-functional requirements.

    - Chapter 4 provisioned a reliable, secure, cloud infrastructure that is auto-scalable, self-healing and minimizes manual administration labor. It provides cost savings (free database tier) and elasticity in relation to the application workloads.

    - Chapter 5 migrated application code and data into the cloud provider infrastructure.

    - Chapter 6 added observability to the cloud deployment, with full-stack logging, monitoring, alerting, and escalation capabilities.

- *Part III: Software Delivery Migration*

  - Chapter 7 provisioned a DevSecOps set of tools that enabled synergy between people, processes, and technologies and provided a foundation for CICD-automated processes.

  - Chapter 8 designed and implemented an automated CICD pipeline for application, data, configurations, and security within GitLab to deploy, upgrade, roll back, and delete software releases.

- *Part IV: Software Operations Migration*

  - Chapter 9 delivered a set of artifacts, such as the migration readiness checklist, the production migration plan, a cloud operations runbook, and a disaster recovery (DR) solution to the finalized production environment.

  - Chapter 10 will demonstrate the methodology and approach to efficient cloud-native operations and cost management in the cloud environment.

Efficient Cloud Operations Process

Accountability for the application's operating costs in the cloud should be assigned to Product and/or Platform teams based on shared responsibility model for application and infrastructure components. This bottom-up approach to assign responsibility for runtime costs is the most optimal, as teams that are running applications have the best knowledge about workload characteristics and possible optimization locations. This familiarity also helps the teams establish efficient cost management; plan workload resources; create and maintain assets inventory; monitor and control utilization rate; create budgets and alerts; and apply manual and/or automated (policy-based or machine learning-based) optimization practices. Given that IT budget reduction is often a primary driver of cloud migration, the approach described here should help. In order to achieve the desired outcome, we recommend the process that consists of the following steps: *plan, organize, monitor, control, and optimize.* This process is depicted in Figure 10-1.

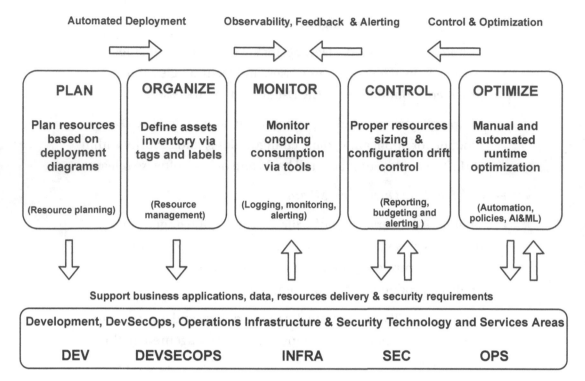

Figure 10-1. Efficient cloud operations process

Plan

This step's objective is to perform upfront planning for cloud resources, properly size services, compute, storage, and networking infrastructure. The output is a detailed, and all-inclusive resource planning document (e.g., an Excel spreadsheet), including VM, CPU, RAM, networking (subnets, security groups, public IP addresses, egress and ingress, data and storage requirements. Typical inputs for this document are deployment diagrams and other cost-related materials for the services, e.g., an Elastic Cloud service pricing list. This plan is then compared to the actual cost after the application is installed in the cloud environment. It is adjusted and refined based on cloud deployments workloads analysis to ensure the provisioned infrastructure meets performance, quality, and storage requirements.

Organize

This step clearly labels, tags, and organizes cloud resources to present a comprehensive inventory to ensure full visibility, accountability, and support for monitoring, controlling, and optimization functions down the road.

Inventory information typically serves multiple stakeholders, such as the Product, Platform, Finance, and Management teams. In the previous chapters, we have introduced cloud resources naming and tagging document that would assist with this task.

There are plenty of helpful resources and templates on the Internet, e.g. the Azure Git Hub Repository (*https://github.com/MicrosoftDocs/cloud-adoption-framework/ blob/master/docs/ready/azure-best-practices/naming-and-tagging.md*) is one such example. More are provided in the "Tools, Techniques, and Best Practices" section later in this chapter.

Monitor

This step is concerned with ongoing monitoring of application workloads and comprehensive, real-time reporting of all incurred cloud costs.

Monitoring, logging (application and infrastructure components), and alerting was provisioned and configured in Chapter 6. Tools include Elastic Cloud (logs), Prometheus and Grafana (metrics), and PagerDuty for alerting. We can produce different kinds of alerts, including application runtime alerts and budget overruns alerts.

Control

Here we establish automated control over application operational characteristics: performance, quality, and cost utilization. We employ best practices, tools, and cloud provider services, including setting thresholds, budgets and automated alerts.

The ultimate purpose of this step is to provide an automated feedback loop to the teams. We introduce cloud reporting and controlling tools, such as AWS Cost Management. Other cloud providers have similar tooling for cost management and reporting. We need to ensure that during this step we capture and correct any configuration, deployment and resource utilization drifts that could lead to cost overruns.

Optimize

Finally, we review and assess performance, cost, and utilization rates of our cloud provider assets. We identify assets that could be optimized and apply *manual, policy-based, or machine learning* optimization steps and activities.

Optimization could include resizing the instance, shutting down unused instances, or buying resources in the spot market for nonpersistent workloads. Each cloud provider offers some kind of cloud advisory service that constantly monitors cost and security resource utilization and provides ongoing feedback via a web console, APIs, or emailed reports. Example of such tools are the AWS Compute Optimizer, the AWS Cost Management Recommendations, and the AWS Trusted Advisor.

Inputs

The following inputs—including application components, infrastructure, and documentation—are required to help establish efficient cloud-native software operations. These artifacts have been delivered throughout the book and are summarized in Chapter 9. They come from Infra and Ops Services and Technology areas to ensure uninterrupted migration continuity in regard to software value delivery blocks and documentation.

- Cloud resources naming and tagging

- AWS EKS Cluster

- AWS PostgreSQL RDS

- Resource capacity and cost planning document

- Disaster Recovery environment

- Cloud operations runbook

- Monitoring, logging, and alerting implementation

  - Prometheus, Grafana deployment

  - Elasticsearch, FluentBit, Kibana deployment

  - PagerDuty environment

- Monitoring, logging, and alerting handbook

- Application migration readiness checklist

- Production migration plan

- Disaster Recovery document

Keep in mind that the list is a baseline; documents and artifacts could vary for each project and should be adopted and extended to match a particular real-life migration scenario, context, or environment.

After all the required inputs are collected, you can move on to the processes and activities section.

Processes and Activities

In this section, we start estimating costs for AWS components using the AWS Pricing Calculator (*https://calculator.aws/#/*). After we establish baseline costs for AWS resources, including AWS EKS Cluster, AWS PostgreSQL RDS, and other infrastructure, we move on to services outside of AWS. We add Elastic Cloud costs using the company calculator and finally PagerDuty costs. Next, we configure budgeting alerts using the AWS Cost Management Tool. Finally we optimize our deployment to reduce overall deployment cost and achieve coveted elasticity that matches application workloads to the provisioned resources.

Organize and Tag for Visibility

To organize cloud AWS resources inventory for the subsequent monitoring and control, we add tags and labels to each resource: AWS EKS Kubernetes Cluster, AWS PostgreSQL RDS, and AWS S3 storage. For brevity we add a single label to demonstrate the concept. Labels could and should be applied automatically as part of the continuous deployment step. Labeling and tagging provides visibility benefits that help organize and view cost per business unit or per Product team. Labeling and tagging could also help validate a variety of accounting items according to the accounting model that exists in a given organization.

Navigate to the AWS PostgreSQL RDS service and open the *Tag* tab. Enter Tags = Environment; Value = PROD. See Figure 10-2.

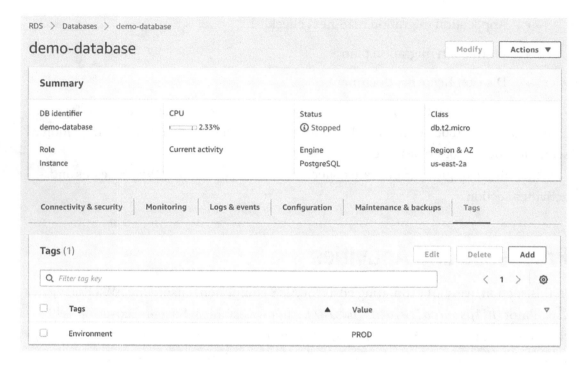

Figure 10-2. *AWS PostgreSQL Service tagging*

Report, Budget and Alert

After cloud resources have been clearly identified and labeled, we can move on to meter the resource utilization and create budgets and alerts to avoid cost runaway. To calculate a total solution of costs for our sample deployment, follow these steps. We find and summarize the costs for the AWS, Elasticsearch, and PagerDuty components that together comprise total cost for our sample solution.

1. Navigate to the *AWS Pricing Calculator*. We add two AWS EKS clusters for brevity and a single AWS PostgreSQL RDS to demonstrate the approach. The total estimate is depicted in Figure 10-3. Add it to Resource Capacity and Cost Planning.

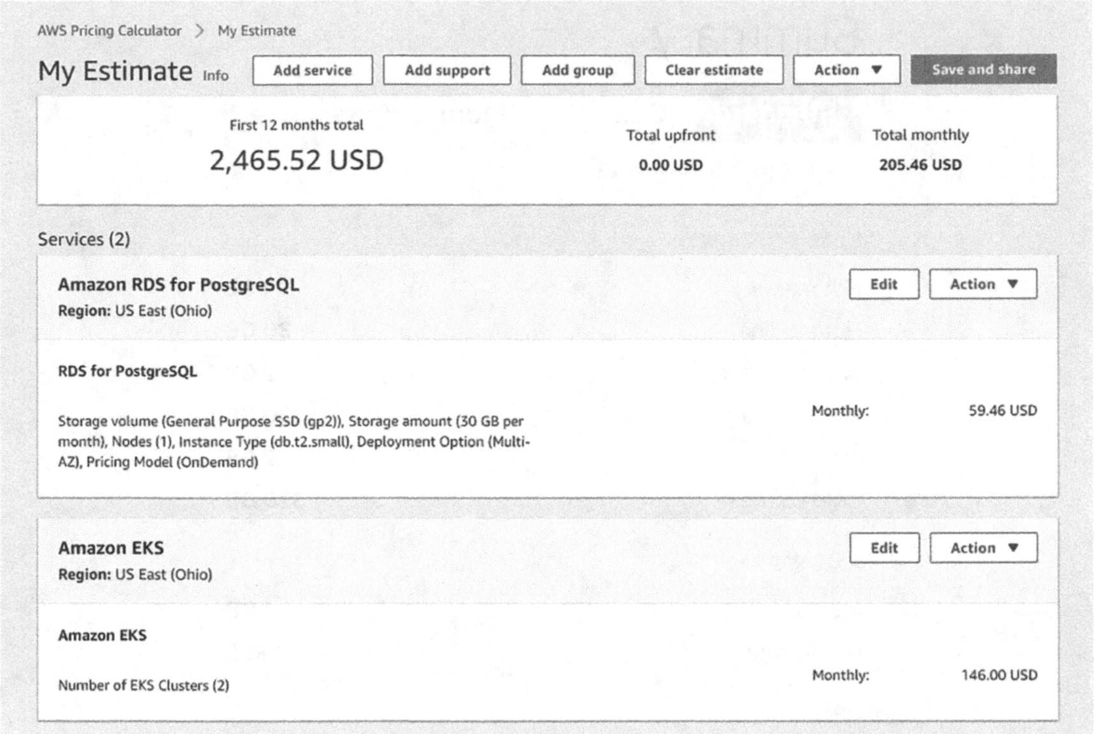

AWS Pricing Calculator > My Estimate

My Estimate Info | Add service | Add support | Add group | Clear estimate | Action ▼ | Save and share |

First 12 months total	Total upfront	Total monthly
2,465.52 USD	0.00 USD	205.46 USD

Services (2)

Amazon RDS for PostgreSQL   Edit | Action ▼
Region: US East (Ohio)

RDS for PostgreSQL

Storage volume (General Purpose SSD (gp2)), Storage amount (30 GB per   Monthly: 59.46 USD
month), Nodes (1), Instance Type (db.t2.small), Deployment Option (Multi-
AZ), Pricing Model (OnDemand)

Amazon EKS   Edit | Action ▼
Region: US East (Ohio)

Amazon EKS

Number of EKS Clusters (2)   Monthly: 146.00 USD

Figure 10-3. *AWS cost estimates*

2. Navigate to the Elastic Cloud Calculator *(https://cloud.*
    elastic.co/pricing). Select an I/O optimized hardware profile
    that will be deployed to AWS cloud. Ensure that you select the
    same region where your AWS resources are already deployed,
    to avoid additional egress traffic charges. In our cases, it's US
    East (Ohio). After selecting the desired CPU, RAM and storage,
    redundancy, as well as storage option and subscription types, you
    can see total estimated cost for the service. The total and hourly
    cost is depicted in Figure 10-4. Add it to Resource Capacity and
    Cost Planning.

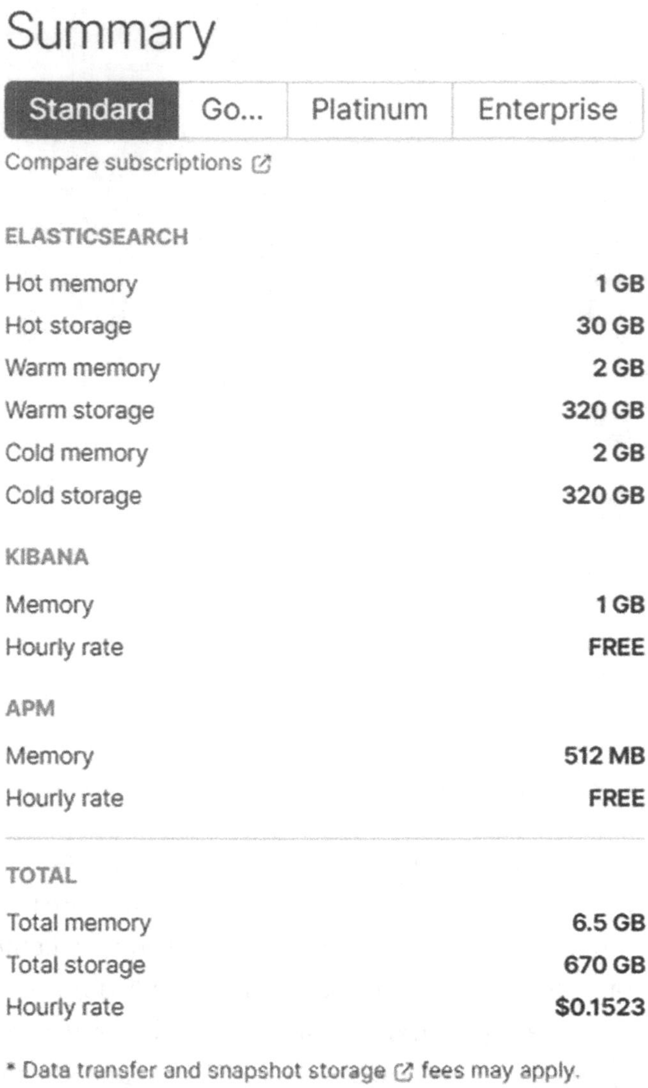

Summary

| Standard | Go... | Platinum | Enterprise |

Compare subscriptions ☑

ELASTICSEARCH

Hot memory	1 GB
Hot storage	30 GB
Warm memory	2 GB
Warm storage	320 GB
Cold memory	2 GB
Cold storage	320 GB

KIBANA

Memory	1 GB
Hourly rate	FREE

APM

Memory	512 MB
Hourly rate	FREE

TOTAL

Total memory	6.5 GB
Total storage	670 GB
Hourly rate	$0.1523

* Data transfer and snapshot storage ☑ fees may apply.

Figure 10-4. *Elastic Cloud cost estimates*

3. Navigate to the PagerDuty *Pricing Page (https://www.pagerduty. com/pricing/)* and review the different pricing plans. There is a wide variety of features to choose from, that can satisfy various team's alerting requirements. For the purpose of this text, select $20 USD/month per user and assume you need five licenses. Add it to Resource Capacity and Cost Planning. See Figure 10-5.

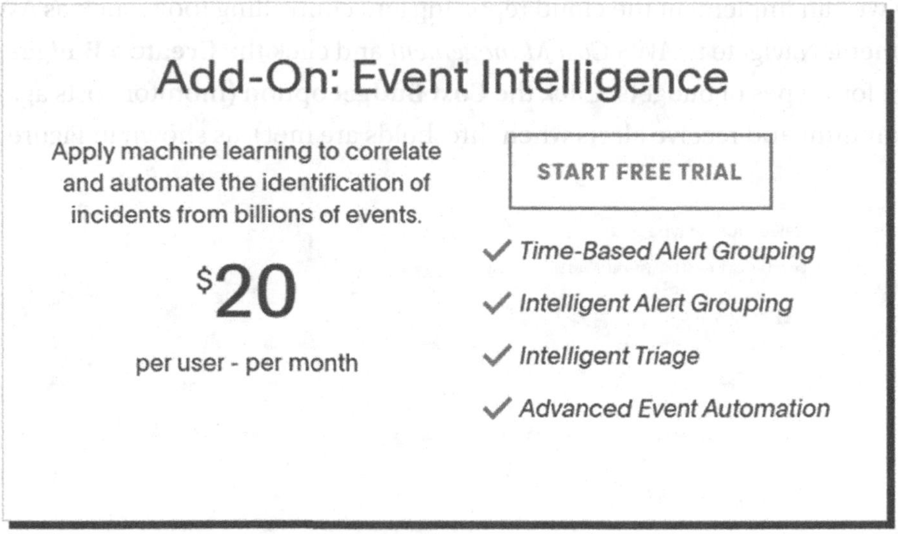

Add-On: Event Intelligence

Apply machine learning to correlate and automate the identification of incidents from billions of events.

START FREE TRIAL

$20

per user - per month

✓ *Time-Based Alert Grouping*

✓ *Intelligent Alert Grouping*

✓ *Intelligent Triage*

✓ *Advanced Event Automation*

Figure 10-5. PagerDuty cost estimates

After all the expenses have been added to the Resource Capacity and Cost Planning document, the single cloud-based instance of the solution will cost an estimated $259.58 USD per month. See Table 10-1 for details. Real-life scenarios are much more complicated. The team need to take into consideration various development, quality assurance, user acceptance testing and disaster recovery environments. Table below simply represents minimalistic model and template on how to approach the total cost calculations across different vendors and services.

Table 10-1. Resource Capacity and Cost Planning

Component	Units	Cost Per Unit	Total
Demo Web application	1 (AWS EKS Kubernetes Cluster)	$125.35	$125.35
Demo business application			
Demo database	1 (AWS RDS service)	$0 (free tier)	$0
PagerDuty	1 (account)	$20	$20
Elastic Cloud	750 (hours)	$0.1523	$114.23
Total			**$259.58**

Now we can implement the cloud reporting and controlling tools, such as AWS Cost Management. Navigate to *AWS Cost Management* and click the **Create a Budget** button. There are four types of budgets. Click the **Cost Budget** option (monitor costs against a specific amount and receive alerts when thresholds are met), as shown in Figure 10-6.

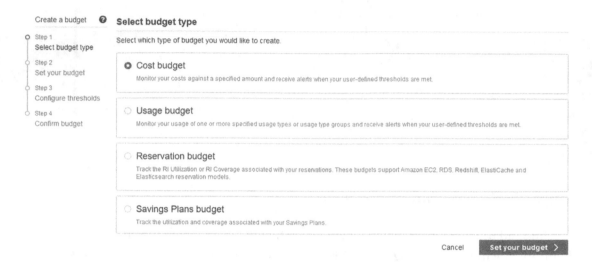

Figure 10-6. *AWS cost management: set your budget*

Next enter the budget name and click the **Configure Threshold** button. Set the threshold amount and add a notification email. There are other options on this page, but we ignore them. Click the **Confirm** Budget button to continue; see Figure 10-7.

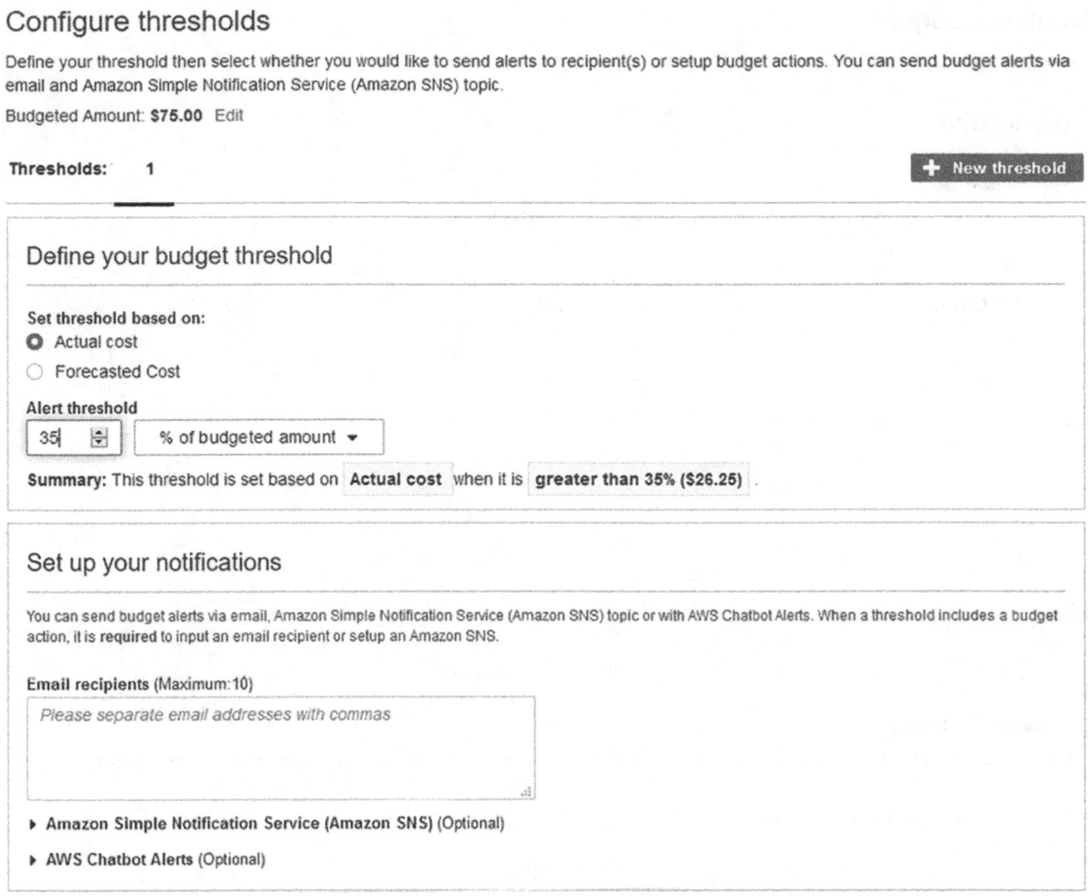

Configure thresholds

Define your threshold then select whether you would like to send alerts to recipient(s) or setup budget actions. You can send budget alerts via email and Amazon Simple Notification Service (Amazon SNS) topic.

Budgeted Amount: **$75.00**   Edit

Thresholds: 1   **+ New threshold**

Define your budget threshold

Set threshold based on:
- ⦿ Actual cost
- ◯ Forecasted Cost

Alert threshold

| 35 | ⬍ | % of budgeted amount ▾ |

Summary: This threshold is set based on **Actual cost** when it is **greater than 35% ($26.25)** .

Set up your notifications

You can send budget alerts via email, Amazon Simple Notification Service (Amazon SNS) topic or with AWS Chatbot Alerts. When a threshold includes a budget action, it is **required** to input an email recipient or setup an Amazon SNS.

Email recipients (Maximum: 10)

Please separate email addresses with commas

▸ **Amazon Simple Notification Service (Amazon SNS)** (Optional)

▸ **AWS Chatbot Alerts** (Optional)

Figure 10-7. *AWS cost management: confirm budget*

At this point, you can review the budget details and click the **Create** button to finalize budget creation, as shown in Figure 10-8.

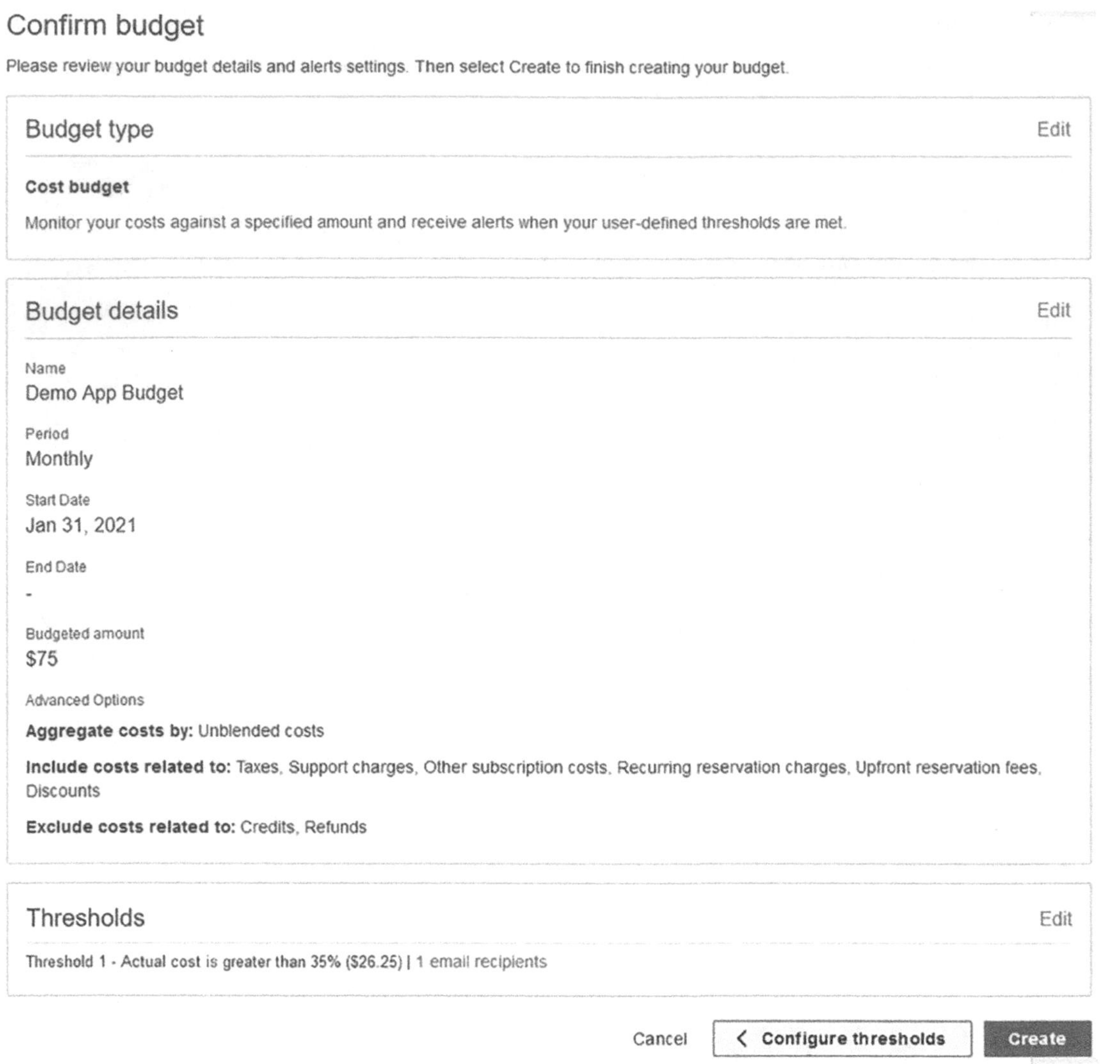

Confirm budget

Please review your budget details and alerts settings. Then select Create to finish creating your budget.

Budget type   Edit

Cost budget

Monitor your costs against a specified amount and receive alerts when your user-defined thresholds are met.

Budget details   Edit

Name
Demo App Budget

Period
Monthly

Start Date
Jan 31, 2021

End Date
-

Budgeted amount
$75

Advanced Options

Aggregate costs by: Unblended costs

Include costs related to: Taxes, Support charges, Other subscription costs, Recurring reservation charges, Upfront reservation fees, Discounts

Exclude costs related to: Credits, Refunds

Thresholds   Edit

Threshold 1 - Actual cost is greater than 35% ($26.25) | 1 email recipients

---

Cancel   ❮ **Configure thresholds**   **Create**

Figure 10-8. *AWS cost management: create budget*

Finish the process by navigating to the **Budget Creation** page. The sample budget shown in Figure 10-9 sends an email alert when the cost linked with Demo App Budget exceeds $26.25 for the current month. Real-life budgets are thousands of dollars and higher. The monthly cost associated with this budget is $32.96. Additional details can be found by accessing the **AWS Budgets** dashboard.

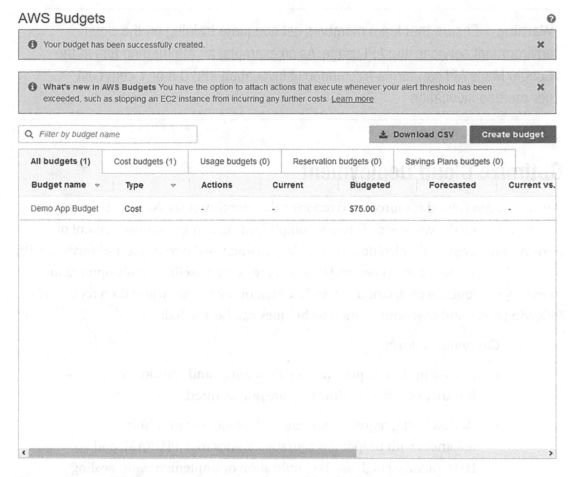

Figure 10-9. *AWS cost management created budget*

This and other similar watermark alerts and reports are extremely important and must be set during cloud migration. It is easy to have cost overruns in the cloud environments, particularly when there is not enough experience or training. We have all read or heard the horror stories, which almost became urban legends, when a free account turns into $7,000 USD/day virtually overnight. This might be due to an inefficient loop algorithm inside the application code that keeps resaving the ever-growing array list and sending it over the network, or a wrong argument flag that was used inside a Google Map API method call, and it caused a 1 cent per invocation charge instead of being free.

Warning   Ensure that team members get adequate training on the cloud environment services and API usage. As an example, an API method flag in the Google Maps API can turn a free endpoint invocation into 0.5 or 1 cent cost per method invocation.

Optimize Cloud Deployment

We have tagged cloud resources and reported the monthly costs. Now it's time to start fine-tuning the workload. This is accomplished via continuous assessment of performance, cost, and utilization rates. First, you identify the resource and services with a low utilization rate or high cost, and this becomes your baseline. Apply optimization tools or techniques to each cloud tier, technology, or service area, and then repeat. The following areas and cost optimization techniques can be applied:

- *Compute resources:*

    - Review uptime requirements for instances and shutdown instances during the time they are not required.

    - Review sizing requirements and utilization and provision instances with proper configuration values for CPU, RAM, and HD to achieve high levels of utilization or implement auto-scaling capability for load elasticity.

    - Review instance terms and match workload requirements to the terms: three years, one year, on-demand, or spot (the cheapest).

- *Data:*

    - Review database components' sizing requirements and utilization and provision instances with proper configuration values for CPU, RAM, and HD to achieve high levels of utilization or implement auto-scaling capabilities for load elasticity.

- *Storage:*

    - Select proper storage class and cost based on value, criticality, durability, and availability requirements.

- Automate migration of data between different storage classes: hot-warm-cold to reduce costs of long-term stored data based on data transfer frequency, retention period, and amount.

- *Networking:*

  - Design cost-efficient component deployment in regard to networking architecture, e.g. cloud providers do not charge for the traffic ingress or traffic between the zones, while egress and intra-region traffic does cost.

Overall approaches vary from using reserved or spot instances, to manually fine-tuning, to policy- or service-based optimization, to machine learning software.

Output and Deliverables

The list of deliverables in this chapter focuses on the operations within cloud production environment. The list below could be extended or adopted to fit particular migration requirements, scenarios, and environments. We started with resource tagging and labeling and resource capacity and cost planning to capture AWS, Elastic cloud, and PagerDuty inventory cost for completeness and visibility. We moved on to an AWS Cost Report and AWS Cost Budget to understand the cost utilization on a monthly basis, as well as to prevent unexpected cost overruns. See the list of deliverables in Table 10-2.

Table 10-2. *Outputs and Deliverables*

Deliverable	Mandatory	Completed	Team
Resource tagging and labeling	Yes	Yes	Product team
Resource capacity and cost planning	Yes	Yes	Product team
AWS cost budget	Yes	Yes	Product team
AWS cost report	Yes	Yes	Product team

Tools, Techniques and Best Practices

This section provides reference materials for cloud-native, cost-efficient software operations (in the Ops technology and services area). The idea behind the list is that these technologies, tools, and techniques are aligned with the cloud migration *design principles* and allow the team to take full advantage of the cloud *deployment model, the cloud services model*, the migration strategies, and the cloud computing characteristics.

The ultimate objectives for the software operations solution, which is also cloud provider's main selling point, is to help the Product and Platform teams match workloads with resources and achieve *cost-to-workload elasticity*, or in simple terms "pay for only what you use." This goal is also aligned with the *Lean Manufacturing* principle, which focuses on eliminating waste from the operational production environment and focuses IT teams on value-added operational activities.

Given the high price of inefficient cloud operations, no pun intended, this area has seen an explosion of models, methodologies, culture change initiatives (e.g. building cost-conscious organizations), techniques, and supportive software tools, including machine learning and artificial intelligence offerings. The list in Table 10-3 provides users with a good starting point in regard to reference materials. It can help you build cost-conscious organizations in the OPS Technology and Services area and develop cost-efficient operations within the cloud provider infrastructure.

Table 10-3. *Tools, Techniques, and Best Practices*

Tool, Technique, or Best Practice	Description/Benefits and Link
Azure cost management	Set of tools provided by Microsoft to report, analyze, and manage workload costs
Azure naming and tagging	Azure naming and tagging strategy
Azure cost management discipline	One of the five disciplines of cloud governance within the Cloud Adoption Framework governance model
Azure cost management discipline template	Template to document and communicate cost management issues
Azure cloud adoption framework: cost conscious organization	Cost-conscious organization approach recommendations by Azure
AWS well architectured framework	Set of tools, labs, and recommendations from AWS to evaluate workloads, identify risks, and record progress of improvements
AIOps	Applying artificial intelligence algorithms and tools to IT operations
Azure cost management automation solutions on GitHub	Cost Management Automation services to retrieve and manage cost data
Kubecost	Kubernetes software tool for cost reporting
Microsoft Azure assessment tools	Set of Microsoft Azure curated assessments

Summary

This chapter presented a practical understanding of the cloud-native operations model, reviewed the building blocks from the previous chapters that contributed to the migration into the cloud environment, and focused on cloud-native operations, in particular—the cost discipline.

It reviewed the cloud cost management model that consists of *plan, organize, monitor, control, and optimize steps,* and discussed the cost-optimization techniques within different groups of cloud provider resources and services. It ensured that cloud spending costs and related metrics are monitored and reported regularly via services supplied by the cloud provider.

The reported cost was then reviewed, analyzed, and optimized within the compute, data, storage, and networking resource groups. This chapter wrapped up with a focus on developing a cost-conscious organization as a critical culture change in order to ensure both successful cloud migration as well as long-term operations process.

Epilogue

Congratulations and thank you dear reader!

I would like to thank you from the bottom of my heart that you have chosen to spend your valuable time reading this book. After you have finished reading this book, I hope you also were able to successfully migrate your application to the cloud provider infrastructure. I trust that this book was on your tabletop every step of the way and helped you answer critical questions during the migration journey or at the very least pointed you in the right direction.

There were a couple of objectives I had in mind when writing this book. First and foremost, the idea was to provide a comprehensive view of the cloud computing world, its characteristics and models, its paradigm changes and related opportunities and challenges. This knowledge will make you comfortable with cloud computing concepts and empower you to use them to your advantage without being burned by the unknowns.

My second objective was to develop critical thinking around cloud computing and being able to objectively evaluate technologies and solutions as well as make sound decisions. This idea was supported by the well structured methodology of the migration process, backed by the sample project code and accompanying environment. This approach and methodology is not only limited to cloud migration; it could be successfully applied to other scenarios.

My third objective was to build a foundational knowledge, a platform of a kind, from which your mind can reliably launch into the open space of the cloud computing universe that you will face in the foreseeable future.

Good luck, dear reader and all the best in your future cloud-native endeavors!

References

Mell, Peter, and Grance Timothy (2011). "The NIST Definition of Cloud Computing." *National Institute of Standards and Technology, US Department of Commerce,* Special Publication 800-145. Retrieved from *https://nvlpubs.nist.gov/*.

Conway, Melvin. E. (1968). How to Committees Invent. *Design Organization Criteria*. Retrieved from *http://www.melconway.com/*.

Index

A

Agile development methodologies, 145
Agile software delivery methods, 144
AIOps, 24, 204, 221
Alert fatigue, 131, 132
Alerting
    deliverables, 133–135
    implementation, 115
    migration application, 132
    PagerDuty, 132
    tools/techniques/best practices, 135–137
Amazon PostgreSQL RDS, 77
Amazon Web Services (AWS), 42, 46, 48,
    51, 54
Application state, 138
Architectural system property, 112
Architecture anti-pattern, 112
Architecture katas, 43
Architecture requirements, 46
Artificial intelligence (AI), 15
Artificial intelligence, 24, 31
Automated pipelines
    AWS database connection, 167
    AWS EKS integration, 167
    build stage, 162, 164
    CICD, 163
    cloud computing, 161
    deliverables, 173–176
    development team, 162
    GitLab

application deployment, 172, 173
    deploy job, 171, 172
    docker-build job, 170, 171
    gitlab-ci.yml, 167, 168
    maven-build job, 169, 170
    pipeline, 169
    gitlab-ci.yml, 166
    release stage, 163, 164
    requirements, 165, 166
    run stage, 163, 165
    tools/techniques/best practices, 177, 178
AWS availability zone, 62
AWS cloud formation, 62, 65
AWS Command Line Interface (CLI), 61, 62
AWS Cost Management Tool, 209
AWS Data Migration Service, 77
AWS Elastic Kubernetes Service (EKS), 46,
    58, 61, 64–67, 73, 76, 78, 80, 82,
    83, 88, 98, 100, 103, 105, 165–167,
    171, 172
AWS IAM service, 51
AWS Identity and Access Management
    (IAM), 63, 64
AWS Management Console, 61, 64, 66, 69
AWS PostgreSQL RDS, 58, 72, 73, 116, 130,
    131, 208, 209
AWS PostgreSQL relational
    database service, 48
AWS RDS, 77, 81
AWS Virtual Private Cloud (VPC), 61–63

© Taras Gleb 2021
T. Gleb, *Systematic Cloud Migration*, https://doi.org/10.1007/978-1-4842-7252-7

Printed in the United States
by Baker & Taylor Publisher Services

Printed in the United States
by Baker & Taylor Publisher Services